Temple Beth David

6100 Hefley Street
Westminster, CA 92683
(714) 892-6623

Hannah Szenes-
 a song of light-

illustrated by Donna Ruff

The Jewish Publication Society
Philadelphia • New York • Jerusalem
5746 • 1986

Hannah Szenes-
a song of light-

by Maxine Schur

Text copyright © 1986 by Maxine Schur
Illustrations copyright © 1986 by Donna Ruff
All rights reserved   First edition
Manufactured in the United States of America

Library of Congress Cataloging in Publication Data

Schur, Maxine.
    Hannah Szenes : a song of light.

    Summary: A biography of the Jewish heroine whose
mission to help rescue European Jews in World War II cost her her life.
        1. Senesh, Hannah, 1921–1944—Juvenile literature.
    2. Jews—Palestine—Biography—Juvenile literature.
    3. Holocaust, Jewish (1939–1945)—Hungary—Juvenile
    literature.   4. World War, 1939–1945—Underground move-
    ments, Jewish—Hungary—Juvenile literature.   [1. Senesh,
    Hannah, 1921–1944.   2. Jews—Biography]   I. Ruff, Donna, ill.   II. Title.
    CT1919.P38S947   1985   940.53′15′039240439 [92]   85–5794

The translations of Hannah Szenes' prose and poetry excerpted here are reprinted by permission
of Schocken Books Inc. from Hannah Senesh: Her Life and Diary, © 1966 by
Hakibbutz Publishing House Ltd.; English edition © 1971 by Nigel Marsh, published by
Schocken Books Inc.

ISBN 0–8276–0251–0

Designed by ADRIANNE ONDERDONK DUDDEN

This book is dedicated to
     ROSA SULTAN-LIPNOWSKA
        1885, Walischbirken–1943, Treblinka

acknowledgments-

Over the past three years, several people helped me write this book. I wish to thank them all.

First, Beverly Gherman for her sympathetic ear and continual encouragement; Arleen Sonnenshine for her devoted attention to detail and astute comments; Shirleyanne Costigan for her keen editorial advice; Rivka Postrel for her time in translating letters from Hebrew; and Miriam Solis for translating the Hungarian letters.

Many kind people encouraged and advised me throughout this project: Peter Hay, Hannah's translator; Miriam Neeman, archivist at S'dot Yam; Magda Zimmering, Hannah's school friend; Ryna Farber, Hannah's teacher at Nahalal; and Penina Aloni and Miriam Pergamot, Hannah's friends.

Above all, I wish to express my gratitude to George and Catherine Szenes for their kindness and generosity in sharing their loving memories of Hannah with me.

In the United States Hannah's last name is most often spelled "Senesh." I have chosen to spell it "Szenes" to retain the original Hungarian spelling.

We gathered flowers in the fields and mountains
We breathed the fresh winds of spring,
We were drenched with the warmth of the sun's
    rays
In our Homeland, in our beloved home.

We go out to our brothers in exile,
To the suffering of winter, to frost in the night.
Our hearts will bring tidings of springtime,
Our lips sing the song of light.

-Hannah Szenes
1944

prologue-

1:00 A.M.
March 13, 1944

The night is beautiful, lit by the silver shimmer of a full moon and the random glitter of the galaxy. On a camouflaged runway in Brindisi, Italy, a British cargo plane takes off. Inside, five young parachutists crouch amid huge bundles of food. They are weighed down by their harnesses, guns, and heavy winter clothes beneath their British uniforms. These young parachutists are not soldiers. They are not British. They're young Jewish farmers from the kibbutzim, the collective settlements of Palestine. Only two months before, they begged the British to let them go on this dangerous assignment—to parachute into Nazi-occupied Yugoslavia and organize the scattered Resistance fighters. Knives are sewn into their shirts, their silk handkerchiefs are drawn with maps, and their shirt buttons are really tiny compasses. On their backs they carry radio equipment, code books, important documents, and bombs. If they fail, if they are captured, they must destroy the documents—perhaps take their own lives.

Hours go by slowly. The thunderous roar of the plane's engines kills almost all conversation. The flight to Yugoslavia will take five hours, but, at first, the parachutists are too nervous to sleep. They talk and laugh wildly, shouting to be heard; then, taking turns, they doze fitfully for an hour or two. One of them does not sleep at all—Hannah Szenes.

Hannah is one of the few women ever to be taken into the British air force, and she's the only female parachutist of this Jewish Resistance group. This green-eyed student from Budapest is just twenty-two, yet she is fulfilling her most cherished dream—to fight the Nazis. Hannah is already known as the most daring of the parachutists. Her courage comes from a deep spiritual conviction that it is her mission in life to help rescue the remaining Jews of Europe, including the million in her native Hungary.

Hour after hour, while the others sleep or talk, Hannah works on a poem: writing, crossing out what she has written, rewriting. Suddenly her stomach jumps. The plane dives low and then circles in the dawn-pink sky, wheeling like a hawk eying its prey. The crew begins hurling food bundles out of the hatch, and the British officer gives the order to jump. The young people line up to be greeted by a blast of icy wind at the open plane door. The faces of the four young men are tense and fearful, but Hannah's face, small and delicate beneath her helmet, seems relaxed, even happy. To the others she looks like a little girl. They smile as she gives them her favorite victory sign, thumbs up. Before she jumps, she shuts her eyes and reminds herself she *must* succeed. Then she hurls herself into the cold sky air, falling, falling, the wind whistling past her ears, pushing into her face, falling as the earth below seems to grow larger, rushing up to meet her. Falling faster and faster while her head spins with a thousand thoughts at once:

> Life is a brief and hurtling day,
> Pain and striving fill every page . . .

Her eyes burning with the wind, she drops yet faster, and her light body is violently blown off course. She's falling sideways!

Faster, faster, faster. Then with a rough, sudden jerk her parachute opens, and for the last few thousand feet Hannah, the Jewish girl poet, floats gracefully into Nazi-held Yugoslavia.

one-

Hungary 1921

Budapest in 1921 was one of the most beautiful cities in the world. The loveliness of the Danube—the wide, gray river that runs through the city—was praised in a dozen love songs. Dotted with islands, laced with bridges, and edged with grand hotels, the Danube was the romantic and commercial center of the city. From the Danube, Budapest extended on either side in elegant chestnut-tree–lined boulevards and twisted cobblestone paths. Tall, modern buildings stood alongside ornate houses with curving iron balconies. And atop the city rose the domes and cupolas of churches.

Strolling gypsy violinists, broad green parks, and the enormous Gothic parliament building fronting on the Danube all reflected the beauty and culture of the city. But it was a façade, a mask that hid the other face, the ugly face, of Budapest.

Budapest was still in shock from the horrible world war that had ended just three years earlier. Seventy percent of Hungary's land had been lost in that war, lost to Czechoslovakia and Romania. Many Hungarians were furious about that loss. They had been robbed of their land. And the war had created terrible unemployment. Angyföld, a poor section of Budapest, was the worst slum in all of Europe. Garbage was piled in the streets. Children dressed in rags cried from hunger. Rats raced through the dark alleyways.

Wealthy noblemen gambled in posh riverside casinos while ragged, jobless men lined the quays with their makeshift poles, fishing for food for their families.

Wealth and beauty coexisting with poverty and squalor, this was the true Budapest of 1921—the Budapest into which Hannah Szenes was born.

For Hannah there was no poverty or squalor. She lived the spoiled, comfortable life of an upper-class Jewish child. For her there was no need to face dirt or hunger. Hannah's life was a round of excursions, treats, and surprises. For her there was no cramped, musty hovel to live in. The Szenes family resided in a large apartment in Rose Hill, a quiet, tree-lined suburb of Budapest.

Catherine Szenes, Hannah's mother, was a tall, elegant woman, shy and gentle. George, Hannah's brother who was only a year older than she, was her best friend and constant playmate. Fini Mama, Catherine's mother who lived with them, was Hannah's confidante, wise and patient. But it was Hannah's father, Béla, whom she adored.

Béla Szenes was the popular, witty columnist of the *Pesti Herlap*, Budapest's main newspaper. And he was a famous comic playwright. When he was still in his twenties, this tall, thin man with the dashing mustache and penetrating blue eyes became the darling of the literary and artistic world of Hungary. The Szenes apartment was the gathering place for Hungary's most famous artists, writers, and actors. Sometimes Hannah stayed up late and caught glimpses of these important people.

Sleepy-eyed yet excited, she loved the whole glamorous scene. Men smoked cigars and talked about Europe's latest plays. Beautiful women waved long cigarette holders and let out soft ripples of laughter. While the young servant girl, Rosika, circled the guests with trays of appetizers and champagne, someone would drift over to the piano and play the latest song from America.

To Hannah and George, Papa was full of energy and strength. But in truth, Béla was desperately ill. He had had rheumatic fever as a child and had been left with a weakened heart. Béla and Catherine lived life for the present, making each day as full and happy as they could. They showed their children a world as happy and carefree as the make-believe world of Béla's romantic comedies.

In the grand, historical city of Budapest, each season brought new amusements for the Szenes family. In winter, when snow frosted the domes and spires of the city and it grew too cold even for ice skating, the Szenes parlor resounded with the laughter of dozens of children. Hannah and George played host to their friends, served them cake and candy while their father told them stories.

When spring came and tourist launches began churning the waters of the Danube, Hannah, George, Mama, and Papa strolled along its stony quay. "Look, Papa! Look at the gulls!" Hannah would shout, skipping ahead of her parents to watch the white birds swoop and dive for herring. As always, Béla indulged his children on these outings. Under the bright parasols and hanging baskets of the crowded riverside cafés, he often treated Hannah and George to whipped-cream pastries.

As the warm Budapest spring turned into stifling hot summer, Hannah counted the days until her family made their yearly trip to Lake Balaton. There, in the calm, clear waters of the largest lake in central Europe, Hannah and George would swim and sail. In the evening, they would walk with Papa along the lake's sandy shore, looking for cormorants and marsh snipes in the tall green reeds. Papa would call Hannah his "Aniko" and create stories to amuse her as they walked.

Hannah never tired of listening to Papa's stories. Each morning she and George would race each other to their parents' bedroom door. Mama would open the door, and the children would rush in to hug her, then jump on the soft quilts of their parents' bed. There, Béla would hold his two children close and tell them tales of adventure and romance woven from Hungarian folklore. The stories were filled with kings, queens, monsters, fairies, and angels. And good always won over bad.

"Please, just *one* more story!" Hannah and George would beg. Papa would laugh and tell just one more and one more and one more. Finally, Mama would lead the children away so Béla could begin his writing.

But one morning in 1927 Hannah and George knocked on their parents' door, and it did not open. They could hear Mama inside crying. A moment later they were led away by Fini Mama. Béla Szenes had died in his sleep of a heart attack. He was thirty-three years old.

The next day, a gray day threatened by black rain clouds, Béla Szenes was laid to rest in the Jewish cemetery. Six-year-old Hannah stood in the drizzle, her tears mingling with the raindrops. Suddenly, Hannah felt Fini Mama pull her gently from the grave. Holding George's hand as well, Fini Mama led the children away.

Hannah glanced back once to see her mother—tall, pretty Mama veiled in black—talking to reporters and relatives. Mama's face was pale and tired.

Fini Mama slowly led the children through the cemetery. Hannah's new white shoes caked with mud as she sank in the puddles. The rain fell steadily now. Suddenly, Fini Mama stopped. She fumbled in her black handbag for a lace-edged handkerchief and wiped Hannah's and George's cheeks. "You are not ordinary children," she said firmly. "You, George, are only seven, but you are now the man of the family. And you,

Hannah, you are just starting school. Both of you must behave quietly because your mother is weak and sad." Fini Mama squeezed their hands. "Now is the time for you to be strong. Remember, you are great children."

Hannah listened to Fini Mama's words. She felt neither strong nor great. "I will not cry aloud," she promised herself, "but I will *never* forget Papa."

In the months following the funeral, Hannah sat in her bedroom and heard the low horns of the tugboats pulling barges on the Danube. She felt the warm river breeze that carried the scent of the sea. She watched the flowers in her family's garden grow bright and big.

Long after George began to play and laugh again, Hannah remained withdrawn. During the day she stayed in her room and played with her dolls. At night she lay in bed and listened to Mama playing Chopin on the piano in the parlor below.

She knew, as her father had often told her, that life was beautiful, but she could no longer feel its beauty. Papa was gone. She would never again laugh at his funny stories, nor feel his scratchy face against her cheek, nor hear him call her his "darling Aniko." Hannah often buried her head in her pillow and cried herself to sleep.

One autumn day Hannah looked out at the garden beneath her bedroom window. Most of the summer flowers hung dead on their stems except for one small rose still unexpectedly fresh and whole. She got an idea. Taking up a pencil and a scrap of paper she wrote:

> I would like to be cheerful but can't
> However I'd like to, however I try,
> The flower has faded in my heart
> That has been blooming these six years past
> And it faded in the seventh
> Just one little bloom has remained
> Telling me there'll still be joy in life
> But never again as it once was . . .

Hannah looked at what she had just written. She did not care whether the writing was good or bad. She liked the way her poem looked and the way it put her in control of her most private feelings. "My poem," Hannah thought, "is mine but also a part of myself!" She grabbed the paper and ran with it to Fini Mama, who copied the poem neatly into a notebook.

Hannah wrote more poems. She felt proud when her teachers told Mama the poems reminded them of the poetry of Béla Szenes. Hannah was happy. Her sadness lifted. Through writing she felt close again to her father. Now they had a bond death could not destroy.

The next time Hannah visited her father's grave, she stood in the shade of the tall tombstone engraved with the writer's symbols—quill pen and a sheet of paper. Silently, she spoke to her dead father: "Papa, I've learned I can write. Like you, I will one day make others happy through my writing." Then, remembering Fini Mama's words at the funeral, she added, "I am not great now, Papa, but one day I will make a difference in the world. One day," Hannah vowed, "I will be great."

two-

Hungary 1934

When Hannah turned thirteen, the Szenes family moved from their apartment in Rose Hill to a house a few streets away. The large villa on Bimbo Street, with its lovely rose garden, became for the next few years a gracious home for Hannah, George, and their many friends.

Hannah and George were very popular. George's handsome face, lively humor, and athletic and musical abilities made him attractive to many girls. Hannah, now tall with large almond-shaped green eyes and soft brown hair, was the nucleus of a wide circle of friends from Bar Maadas, the exclusive girls' school she attended.

In summer, Hannah loved to swim with George at the large city pools and to hike with him in the Buda hills. At Dombóvár, near Lake Balaton, Hannah loved to talk, swim, and bicycle with her best friend, her cousin Evi.

In winter, Hannah loved to ski down Schwab Hill and skate under the stars. She danced at the Christmas parties of her friends and sang at the Hanukkah parties of her family.

On snowy afternoons, when the houses of Budapest wore thick shawls of snow, Hannah loved to sit for long hours in Fini Mama's bedroom. There Hannah would listen to her grandmother's stories of her childhood in rural Hungary. As the two talked, Fini Mama taught Hannah how to make beautiful Hanukkah gifts—bookmarks, handkerchiefs, and dolls from scraps and rags.

And all year round, Hannah loved to cry with her girlfriends at Greta Garbo movies and laugh with her family at performances of her father's comedies.

But most of all, Hannah loved to write.

As soon as Mama and George were out of the house and it was peaceful, with only Rosika cooking or Fini Mama sewing, Hannah would sit at her little desk and write poems.

"You are very serious," George teased her whenever she refused his invitations to a basketball game or a swim meet.

"Sports are not everything," Hannah would reply.

When she was thirteen, Hannah joined the Literary Society at her school. At first, she was too embarrassed to read her poems in front of the other girls. But at last, at one meeting, she plucked up her courage and read. The other girls liked her poem so much she read another, then another, and another. Soon, Hannah began to live for the Wednesday-afternoon meetings, thirsting for the advice and encouragement of the other girls.

But one day Mama said, "I can't afford to send you to Bar Maadas anymore, Aniko. If the principal does not agree to lower the tuition, you'll have to leave."

Leave Bar Maadas? Leave all her friends and leave the Literary Society? Hannah hated the idea, yet she also hated the tuition rules of the school. The school was Protestant. Catholics paid double the normal tuition. Jews paid triple.

The next day Mama talked to the principal. When she returned from the visit, she told Hannah, "I spoke to all of them—your principal and your teachers—and I told them exactly what I thought. I said, 'In any other school my daughter would have been awarded a scholarship, but in this one I'm paying three times the fee! Because of this injustice, no matter how high your school standards, I'm forced to enroll Hannah somewhere else.' But at these words, Aniko, one of your teachers said, 'No, she is our finest student. She sets the example for the entire school!' At last, the principal said that because of your excellent school work we may pay a double tuition rather than a triple, even though we are Jews."

Hannah was pleased. She knew Mama was usually timid, and so it had taken a great deal of courage for her to speak up. "But Mama," she asked, "why did they make the triple-tuition rule for Jews in the first place? Why do so many people dislike us?"

Hannah's mother reflected a moment before saying, "It is not so much that they dislike us, Hannah. It is that they have been taught to distrust us. Even Papa, as famous as he was, could not have his plays performed at the National Theatre because he was Jewish."

"But the people love Papa's plays!"

"They do, Aniko, but that's the law. Miklós Horthy, our regent, is influenced by all the anti-Jewish slogans going around the cafés of Germany. He is ready to believe the crazy anti-Jewish propaganda of Adolf Hitler. Horthy and some parliament members are saying we made Hungary lose the last war."

"But, Mama, Hungarian Jews fought *for* our country!"

"True, but we are accused of being friendly with France, England, and the United States—the countries that forced Hungary to give up so much land after the war."

"Horthy and those men are telling lies," Hannah said vehemently.

"Yes, Aniko, but people will believe lies if no one will give them the truth."

Hannah reflected on Mama's words and was troubled. Now she understood the changes she had seen recently in her beloved Budapest. German Nazis in brown shirts and swastika armbands stood on the street corners in downtown Pest shouting, "Rid Hungary of the Jewish Menace!" Radio programs discussed the bad influence of the Jews in Hungary. The rich claimed that the Jews endangered Hungary's traditional life style with their communist ideas. The poor claimed that the Jews wanted to set up an elite society that would exclude hard work.

Everywhere Hannah went—on the train, on the streetcars, and in the cafés—she saw people reading the same newspaper. Published by the Hungarian Society for the Extermination of Noxious Insects, the paper's headlines blazed: THE JEWS MUST BE RELEGATED TO AN INFERIOR ROLE FOR THEY ARE AN INFERIOR RACE.

In the cafés at the bottom of Rose Hill, Hannah's neighbors spoke in hushed voices of the latest cruelties the Jews suffered in Germany. Since Hitler had come to power the year before, 1933, life for the Jews there had gotten progressively worse.

Now in Germany, Jews were not considered citizens. They had no right to free speech. They could not attend a meeting, vote, get aid in a hospital, or buy food and drugs in most stores. Every day riots broke out in Germany. Synagogues were burnt. Jewish religious objects were smeared with dung. Innocent Jews were murdered.

"At least in Hungary the Jew is still free," Hannah heard many times. But she also heard Mama say that the present atmosphere in Hungary was warlike. Hannah listened closely to the Jews who spoke with fear in their voices. "There's too much friendliness between Hungary and Germany," these Jews said. "Hitler promised to help Horthy regain Hungary's lost territories, but what does he want in return? He wants Horthy to make the same anti-Semitic laws as those now in Germany! Hitler wants the Jews in return!"

This talk frightened Hannah. One Friday afternoon, she and George took the bus down to the Vérmező, Budapest's enormous public square. It was the fifteenth anniversary of Ad-

miral Miklós Horthy's rise to power as regent of Hungary. George led his sister through the shouting, pushing crowds. At last, standing on her tiptoes and peering around shoulders, she caught a glimpse of the parade.

Thousands of uniformed soldiers marched through the huge square pounding the cobblestone pavement with their heavy black boots. Rifles held tightly in their arms, the soldiers were only boys—teenagers. The crowds screamed in excitement. Some members of the Hungarian fascist party, the Arrow Crossers, came holding up banners praising Hitler. The balconies of the nearby apartment buildings were filled with spectators. Women fainted from emotion; others cried with happiness. Clutching their mothers' skirts, even toddlers carried small Hungarian flags. Almost everyone threw flowers at the passing soldiers.

Suddenly, Hannah felt a cold fear as she watched the soldiers. "It's a good thing George is still too young," she thought as she looked at her brother, imagining him in a uniform. As the cheers of the crowd grew louder and wilder, Hannah wanted to run away and cry, but she stayed with her brother. "God protect us from war," she prayed.

As the months went by, Hannah yearned to discuss the awful things she saw. She took a weekly Bible class with other Jewish students at Bar Maadas, but the teacher—wise and gentle Upor Gyorguy Neni—spoke to them of prayers and ancient history, not of the present problems of the Jews. Hannah's school friends certainly did not want to talk of depressing subjects—they wanted to discuss hair styles and parties. Even Evi, who loved her dearly, did not understand Hannah's seriousness.

By the time school started in the fall of 1934, Hannah knew many of her thoughts had to be kept to herself. She liked the idea of a secret place to record them, so she bought an extra notebook and began a diary. But before she wrote even one word, she vowed that her diary would *never* be like those of other girls her age, full of descriptions of party dresses and gossip. No. Her diary would be a special place, the only place where she could express her thoughts and feelings.

First, Hannah wanted to record all the strong feelings she had about her father. In one of her earliest entries, she wrote:

> I can hardly remember Daddy (his face) but just the same I love him very much and always feel he is with me. I would like to be worthy of him as a writer too. I know I have a little talent ... perhaps through writing I will be able to contribute something toward human happiness.

On that same page, Hannah carefully copied a poem she had written the past summer:

> Life is a brief and hurtling day
> Pain and striving fill every page
> Just time enough to glance around
> Register a face or sound
> And—life's been around.

The poem conveyed her despair over her father's brief, busy life and her belief that life must be lived fully, not wasted. She *would* make a difference.

After she copied it, Hannah read her poem over and over again. Then, because she feared George might find the diary and tease her about it, Hannah closed her diary and hid it under her mattress.

three-

Hungary 1937

During the summer of 1937, the worsening situation for the Jews touched upon Hannah's life. In the past, Hannah's summer visits to her cousin Evi at Dombóvár had been carefree and filled with fun. The two girls had talked, swam, and danced with the boys whose families stayed at the lakeside resorts surrounding Lake Balaton. This summer was different. Although there were boys everywhere, none would come near them. Puzzled by the strange behavior, it soon became evident that the girls were being ostracized—shut out where once they had been welcomed. None of the boys wanted to be seen talking to or even *looking* at a Jewish girl. The two girls were experiencing anti-Semitism firsthand.

In the lakeside resorts of Siófok, Földvar, and others, Jews and Christians were now segregated—on the beaches, in the hotels, and on the dance floors. NO JEWS PLEASE the signs read, or CHRISTIAN HUNGARIANS ONLY.

Hannah and Evi watched as people, who only a year ago had mingled easily, now side-stepped each other. Many Jews said this segregation was a temporary flare-up of anti-Semitism that would soon subside. George ignored it, and Mama talked hopefully of change. But Hannah thought differently. She wrote in her diary:

> This segregation often seems comical but actually it's a very sad and disquieting sign.

Only a week after Hannah returned from Dombóvár, Fini Mama died. All of Hannah's thoughts about the summer past were momentarily put aside. The sudden death of her beloved grandmother allowed Hannah little time for such worries and even less time to cry. Mama herself was so sad and upset that Hannah had to care for her as well as contact relatives and arrange the funeral. Only at night, when she lay alone in her bed, did Hannah cry. Burying her head in her pillow, she grieved over the wise, patient woman who had taught her to make beautiful gifts from scraps and had cherished even Hannah's most awful poems.

The loss of her grandmother at first filled Hannah with overwhelming sadness. But later that summer, Hannah found comfort in remembering that the earth has a natural and beautiful order to it and that death was a part of that order. She wrote a poem, "Evening," to express her love of this beauty and order. Hannah believed it to be the best poem she had ever written and hoped to enter it in the Literary Society's competition in the fall—if she could.

Hannah remembered remarks she had heard last spring that Jewish girls may no longer be allowed to be officers at Bar Maadas. She had hopes of being elected an officer in the Literary Society. Would last semester's remarks become rules this year?

On the first day of the new school year, in September 1937, Hannah walked briskly to school. Underfoot, fallen chestnut leaves crunched loudly, birds sang in the high branches of trees, and puffy white clouds raced across the blue sky. She had always loved to walk through Rose Hill to Bar Maadas.

How many times she had giggled with her friends along the quiet, elegant streets. The view of the Danube from the hilltops was so breathtaking, she had sometimes sang her favorite opera arias aloud to the birds, the trees, and the river.

Now she walked alone. Dressed in the black tights, blue skirt, and blue-checked blouse of her school uniform, she nearly ran through the streets, indifferent to the beauty of the day. She was reciting "Evening" over and over in her head as she walked. She hoped the remarks of last spring would be forgotten. More than anything, she wanted to be accepted in the society. But as she neared the iron gate of her school, she suddenly felt afraid. "Whatever happens," she vowed to herself, "I won't lose my pride."

When Hannah walked into the first meeting of the Literary Society, her spirits were immediately buoyed by the friendly smiles of the other girls. One of the officers of the society was traditionally chosen by the seventh form, Hannah's class. To Hannah's great pleasure, her classmates chose her. At once, the older students in the society rebelled.

"A Jewish student cannot hold office!" the president of the eighth form announced to Hannah's class. "You must hold a new election."

Hannah sat through the new election, trying hard not to cry, trying hard to control the terrible anger that welled up inside her. In a few moments, her class elected Maria, a Christian girl, to be officer. With tears in her eyes, Maria walked over to Hannah.

"I won't accept the appointment because I am not deserving of it. Hannah, you are the one who should have it."

The girls watched in silence as Hannah stood up and looked at Maria. "Accept it calmly," Hannah said, trying to control her voice, "and don't think for an instant that I begrudge you it. Not at all. If you don't accept it, someone else will. After all, it has nothing to do with whether Hannah or Maria is more capable of fulfilling the assignment, but whether a person is a Jew or a gentile."

Hannah walked out of the meeting. Some of the girls and a few teachers followed her, trying to comfort her. But Hannah would not talk to anyone. She didn't care what they thought of her. She didn't care about them or their excuses and explanations. The awful reality of anti-Semitism had been brought home to her. "Now," she said bitterly to herself as she ran home, "now I know what it means to be a Jew in a Christian society."

At home Mama saw her sorrow and urged Hannah to tell her what happened. Hannah told Mama the painful story and then went to her room. There she cried bitterly to herself. At last she took out her diary and wrote:

September 16, 1937
I don't want to take part in or have anything to do with the work of the Literary Society, and don't care about it anymore.

Then to comfort herself, she re-read the poem the Literary Society would never see.

Mildly descends the quiet night,
For earth I know that is right,
The routine of each evening.

A bird is singing in a tree,
The eye of God rests on me.
From the tall sky somewhere.
How infinite this is and great
So bright and awesome—I'm dazed
At the sweetness and loveliness:
A spirit and an immense Being
Guards me through life's wandering
And forever on my ways.

four-

Hungary 1938

Sitting in the waiting room of the *Nyugat*, the most important literary magazine in Hungary, Hannah smoothed her skirt and made a last-minute check of the poems typed and stapled together in her folder. Seventeen-year-old Hannah was both nervous and excited, for in a few minutes Piroska Reichardt, one of the leading journalists of the paper, would be reading her poetry.

When at last told to go into Miss Reichardt's office, Hannah suddenly panicked. But Miss Reichardt smiled warmly and said she was very interested in seeing the writings of the daughter of the famous Béla Szenes.

Hannah sat in silence as Miss Reichardt read each of her poems slowly. At last she looked up.

"The poems surprise me," she said. "You are talented, and these poems are definitely better than average. Yes, I think you will become a writer, though perhaps not necessarily a poet. You're not entirely lyrical, my dear, and your poems have many faults. First, they are apt to be too long, and I feel you compromise the form for the sake of content. Also, sometimes your manner of expression is rather immature. But on the whole, Miss Szenes, I find you talented."

Hannah floated out of Miss Reichardt's office. The July sky was very blue, the Danube especially dazzling. "I have talent!" she said over and over to herself as she made her way across the Grand Boulevard of Pest. "I have talent. Piroska Reichardt thinks I have talent!" She could not wait to tell Mama and George. Hannah raced through the streets in a cloud of happiness.

But Hannah soon came down from her cloud. She may have talent, but if she could not even hold office in her school, how could she ever hope to write professionally? Every day thousands of Jews were being fired from jobs, and Hannah heard her mother's friends say the situation would get even worse. One day, they warned, Jews would not be allowed to work at all.

Hannah toyed with the idea of going away, perhaps to Switzerland or to England. George was planning to study textile production in Austria.

But on March 11, 1938, Hitler changed their plans. On that day Hitler's armies invaded Hungary's next-door neighbor Austria. Hitler was driven into Vienna in a car surrounded by his own Nazi police in black uniforms. At this triumphal parade, many Austrians cheered wildly. Others stood silently in terror.

Seeing Austria collaborate with their enemy, Austrian Jews rushed to leave the country. Cars and taxis jammed the road to Hungary and Czechoslovakia. Hundreds of Jews squeezed into the trains, crammed among the boxes and bags of possessions they had managed to drag with them.

But few Austrian Jews got out. The Nazis ordered the borders closed and stopped the trains from leaving. On the last train that left for the Czechoslovakian border, hundreds of Jewish men, women, and children were beaten, robbed, and dragged off to camps before the train even started. Those who had reached the borders were turned back at gunpoint.

Back in Vienna, the Jews who remained were at once forced to clean the gutters while Nazi storm troopers and the local Austrians jeered at them. Thousands more were made to clean the toilets for the Nazis and then were thrown in jail. Their homes, money, and jewelry were confiscated.

With the invasion of Austria, the Nazi terror was brought to Hungary's doorstep. Everywhere Hannah went—at parties, in school, at her friends' homes—she heard Jews worry over Hitler's next move. "What," they asked, "does the invasion of Austria mean for us? Will Horthy stand up to Hitler?"

Hannah tried to put the questions out of her mind. She read and tried to write poetry, but no matter where she went she found escape impossible. She neglected her diary, going weeks without writing a word. At last, she wrote:

> One is so nervous about the local situation that by the time it comes to writing about things, one feels too depressed and discouraged.

Then in May the situation of the Jews in Hungary suddenly worsened. The First Anti-Jewish Bill was passed in parliament. Called the "stone that began the landslide" for Hungarian Jews, it made Hungary an ally in spirit with the murderous Nazis.

"It is our national duty to keep the Jews in the background," the bill declared. It restricted Jewish participation in business and the professions to only 20 percent. Thousands of Jews found themselves jobless and without any hope of finding work. Many committed suicide.

With the passing of the First Anti-Jewish Bill, anti-Jewish actions became more acceptable and more public. After school at Bar Maadas, many Christian girls formed groups to taunt and spit at the Jewish girls as they walked by. Teachers spoke openly about the destructive spirit of the Jews.

George, now eighteen, decided to leave Hungary rather than run the risk of being drafted. He would go to France, to Lyons, to study textile production.

A month before George left, he appealed to some Hungarian Nazis—Arrow Crossers—in his class to take care of Mama and Hannah should there be any violence against the Jews in Budapest. George thought the bond of school friendship would be enough to make them care for his family. It wasn't. "We cannot help you or your family in any way," they told him coldly.

George was crushed, but Hannah was shocked at George's innocence. Asking Arrow Crossers to take care of them, indeed! Didn't he know they worshiped Hitler? And yet, when she thought of her brother—his boyish face and his concern for Mama and her—Hannah felt she had never loved him more.

It was a clear summer day when Mama and Hannah boarded George's train to say good-by. Hannah tried to appear cheerful. Her big brother—the boy who tried to peek in her diary, who teased her about her boyfriends, and who once wrestled her to the floor in the new grip he had learned at school— was now leaving. Hannah's heart filled with words of love and sadness at the parting, but she could not speak them. The words remained locked inside her, imprisoned by her shyness. Instead, she giggled and joked with him, and George joked back. His handsome face looked untroubled. And his laugh, cutting through the clamor of the train, was loud— almost happy.

"Your new tennis racket is a beauty!" Hannah said. "And so is your suntan."

Hannah teased him about his girlfriends. She quizzed him on his fluency in French and Italian. She gossiped about their mutual friends. Suddenly, the train jerked and the visitors began to leave. Mama hugged George, her eyes brimming with tears; but Hannah only gave George a hurried kiss, then left the train.

On the platform, as the train slowly moved out of the station, Hannah, in desperation, shouted to George about the length of a swimming pool she'd once seen.

"It's really the most enormous pool there is!" she cried.

In a few seconds George's face at the window moved beyond their sight, and in a minute the train itself was gone. Their little family would never be the same again.

Later, alone in her room, Hannah was overwhelmed with sadness. When would she see George again? He was gone, yet the words in her heart were still there. So she put them in her diary:

> You left. We waved a long while
> Porters clattered behind.
> We watched and you disappeared.
>
> Life took you. You were happy.
> Maybe your heart had songs within.
> Our tears were well hidden.
>
> Wordless, we went home.
> Watching the sky, pale and blue,
> And our soul, unseen and secretly,
> Is waving still to you.

five-

In the summer of 1938 Hungary's regent, Admiral Miklós Horthy, vacationed on Hitler's yacht. Hitler told Horthy he was
about to invade Czechoslovakia, Romania, and Yugoslavia.
He said he was willing to give a great deal of this territory
to Hungary if Hungary helped him in the takeover. Hitler
focused his cold brown eyes on Horthy. "He who wants to
sit at the table," he said, "must help in the kitchen."

The temptation was great. After the humiliating territorial
losses Hungary suffered in the First World War, taking over
this land would be sweet revenge. Horthy agreed to help
Hitler. At once Horthy warned his people there would be a
war and called for the mobilization of troops. Throughout
Budapest practice air-raid sirens shrilled, while hoards of un-
employed men lined up waiting to be given uniforms. On the
radio, news bulletins called for donations and volunteers, and
in schools all over Hungary teachers held special services so
pupils could pray for Hungary's swift victory.

Hannah did not want to talk of the ugly and frenzied war

preparations. She preferred to be alone. On Yom Kippur, the Jewish Day of Atonement, she refused even to go to synagogue. Instead she stayed in her room. She brooded on what her Hungarian history teacher had said that week: "The Jews are parasites of the society. They are generally lazy and motivated by greed; they want only to reap the rewards of others." Hannah had listened to these lies in silence, but now it was time to discover the truth. On Yom Kippur Hannah opened the glass bookcases in her parents' study and took out all the books dealing with Jewish history. She read of the richness and glory of Jewish history and of the persecution of the Jews from Biblical times through the Middle Ages and up to 1938. The more she read the more excited she became. She learned all Jews not in Palestine were called "Diaspora" Jews— Jews "dispersed" in foreign lands. Hannah realized that dispossessed of their homeland, the Diaspora Jews inevitably became the victims and scapegoats of their host countries.

What moved Hannah the most was reading the books of Theodor Herzl, a Jew born in Budapest. Herzl wrote that the Jews should return to Zion, their ancient land in Palestine, to create a nation once again. This belief was called Zionism and had gained much support throughout Europe. On October 27, 1938, Hannah wrote:

> I don't know whether I've already mentioned that I've become a Zionist. This word stands for a tremendous number of things. To me it means that I now consciously and strongly feel I am a Jew and proud of it. My primary aim is to go to Palestine and work for it.

Zionism became for Hannah the idealistic mission through which at last she could make a difference in the world.

> One needs something to believe in ... one needs to feel that one's life has meaning, that one is needed in this world. Zionism fulfills all this for me.

From the time Hannah discovered Zionism, she lived in a world distant from her mother, boyfriends, classmates, and even herself—the Hannah she used to be. She was no longer interested in tennis, dancing, boys, or even school. She was no longer the aspiring Hungarian writer. She was a Zionist, sharing her dream with all who would listen, converting the few Jewish girls in her school to its cause.

For her Bible class Hannah wrote a powerful essay, "The Roots of Zionism," in which she tried to share her dream of a new Jewish nation. Standing in front of the handful of girls who were still allowed to study their Jewish past at Bar Maadas, Hannah read the essay in her strong, passionate voice:

> Jewry is living under unnatural conditions, unable to realize its noble characteristics, to utilize its natural talents and capabilities. Thus it cannot cultivate its natural and immortal attributes or fulfill its destiny.
>
> It is not true that during the Dispersion we have become teachers of the people, leaders. On the contrary, we have turned into imitators, servants, become the whipping boys for the sins and errors of those among whom we live....
>
> Even today, in its mutilated form, Palestine is big enough to be an island in the sea of seemingly hopeless Jewish destiny, an island upon which we can peacefully build a lighthouse to beam its light into the darkness, a light of everlasting human values, the light of the one God.

She joined the Hungarian Zionist Youth Society, where she sought out those who had been to Palestine. She made them tell her about what they had seen there. They told her of the commune, or "kibbutz," the life of the pioneers and their ambitious, nearly impossible, agricultural projects to make the dry land bloom. Their words filled her head with clear, powerful images of the place she already loved. She saw a hilly, rough land squeezed between sea and desert; a poor, brittle land, dry and often unbearably hot. Yet in this land Zionists were struggling to make the earth fertile again. Along the malaria-infested Valley of Jezreel irrigation canals had been dug, citrus orchards planted, and swamps drained. From the breezy port city of Haifa in the north to the parched Negev desert in the south, young Jews from all over the world were making their ancient nation live. Hannah saw herself as one of them: shovel or pick in hand, working on the land, sweating in the sun, tired but happy and free.

Hannah wrote to George at the University of Lyons about her dream. To her great surprise, she found that he, too, had become a Zionist! He announced he was already studying Hebrew and intended to immigrate to Palestine.

At Easter, Hannah and Mama went to visit George in France. The two young Zionists talked excitedly about their plans to go to Palestine.

"I want to emigrate to Palestine in a few months, right after graduation," Hannah proclaimed.

"I'll follow you in the fall when I finish my studies" was George's enthusiastic reply.

In the tiny, cramped apartment in the bustling French city, brother and sister talked late into the night, sharing the dream of a Jewish nation thousands of miles away.

six-

Hungary 1939

In February 1939, Horthy appointed a new prime minister for Hungary, Count Pál Teleki. Like the German Nazis, Teleki thought of the Jews as an inferior and dangerous race. "You can in eight or nine cases out of ten recognize a Jew," he liked to boast. Teleki wasted no time in convincing parliament that the Jews were a threat to Hungary. He urged a Second Anti-Jewish Bill to further restrict them.

The time was right for Teleki. Influenced by the pro-German newspapers, the Hungarian people had grown distrustful of the Jews. Jews were blamed for everything from stealing children to poisoning water. In Kisvárda the Jews were said to be running a secret anti-Hungarian radio station, while in Mátészalka they were accused of supplying aircraft to Czechoslovakia.

In March, the Hungarian parliament passed the Second Anti-Jewish Bill. It said:

- Jews cannot hold government positions
- Jews cannot be editors, publishers, writers, play directors, or producers

- Jews cannot teach in primary or secondary schools
- Jews cannot obtain business licenses
- Jews cannot buy or sell land without special government permission

Soon after this law was passed, Hannah graduated with highest honors from Bar Maadas. But the honors meant little to her. Eighteen and burning with only Zionist dreams, she had written an application in Hebrew to the Nahalal Girls School of Agriculture in Palestine and now nervously awaited a reply. Some of the teachers, who had come to love Hannah, were shocked by her idea of leaving Hungary. They appealed to her mother: "Your daughter graduated *summa cum laude*, and though now it is nearly impossible for a Jew to get into a university, we will do everything we can to see that Hannah gets in."

But when Mama told this to her, Hannah answered: "Perhaps I ought to be impressed that in view of graduating *summa cum laude* and with a plethora of recommendations from teachers and friends, I can get into a university, while a gentile who just barely squeezed through exams sails in!"

Then Hannah's mother tried another tactic. She warned her daughter of the hardships she would face in Palestine: "The people there are different from you. You are used to comfort. You crave privacy. They live by sharing totally. They have little time for intellectual pursuits. You thrive on books and intellectual conversations. Hannah, think it over!"

And Hannah replied only with the question, "Who will work the soil, if not the youth?"

She spent the mornings in her room studying Hebrew. In the afternoon, she worked in the garden weeding and planting in the hot sun so she would be used to outdoor work when she came to Palestine.

On July 21, 1939, four days past her eighteenth birthday, Hannah received a letter of acceptance to the Nahalal Girls School of Agriculture.

"I've got it! I've got it! I've got the certificate. I'm filled with joy and happiness!" she wrote in her diary.

For two months Hannah ran to travel agencies, the office of Jewish-Hungarian Aid, and the Palestine Consul. She had her suitcases packed, her passport, her money, and her visa. But on September 1, 1939, Hitler's armies invaded Poland. Poland's allies, England and France, entered the war against Germany. The horrible war everyone had feared had begun.

Hannah was told a sea journey at this time would be dangerous. Few boats would be sailing to Palestine. But Hannah begged to go. Nothing would stop her. She pleaded with officials and travel agents, waiting in lines for hours with hundreds of other Jews wanting to leave Europe. Finally, Hannah was told she could go, but only if she were willing to leave on a Romanian ship. She would need to be at the East Railway Station at noon the very next day.

Hannah and Mama spent all night getting ready. The next morning Hannah tried to act lighthearted. She laughed and chatted easily with Evi and her other relatives who had come to the house to say good-by. But when the relatives left and it was time for Mama and Hannah to head for the station, a deep sadness suddenly filled Hannah.

As they walked through the little iron gate of their house, Hannah looked back just once at the large old house surrounded by trees and flowers. She and George had chased each other up and down the stairs here. Mama had played Chopin late into the night here. This was where Papa's picture hung next to the china cabinet. Fini Mama had died here. And this was where Mama would now live . . . alone.

Hannah turned away from the house, trying to stifle the powerful emotions that swirled within her. But it was useless. Suddenly sobbing uncontrollably, she hugged the faithful Rosika. "Take care of Mama," she cried. "Take care of Mama."

Amid the noise and bustle of the East Railway Station, Mama stood on the windy platform waving up at the sad face in the train window. Though Hannah was smiling as she waved, Mama could see that her face was streaked with tears. At last the train gave out a piercing shriek and began to move slowly out of the station. Hannah's mother watched the train until it disappeared, then walked home through the cool twilight.

The sky was darkening. It was Rosh Hashanah, the Jewish New Year. The iron gate of the house closed behind Mama with a cold, hollow sound. Inside, the house was empty and dim. Mama lit two candles to welcome the New Year. She watched the flames flicker nervously in the shadows of the dark, silent walls.

Somewhere to the east, with every rhythmic clack of the train, a young woman was rushing toward her dream.

seven -

Palestine 1939

The Romanian ship slid into the port of Haifa. In the clear autumn sun, the tired, excited passengers lugged their baggage down the rusty metal gangplank. Hannah Szenes was one of the first to disembark. Her green eyes glowed with happiness as she carried her suitcase and typewriter down the stairs. She was here—in Palestine, land of all her hopes. In her new patent-leather shoes she gingerly stepped over the sea-water puddles along the wharf. She gazed up at the hundreds of little white houses and apartment buildings that dotted the hills of Haifa. She had not expected this harbor city to be so lovely.

At last she reached the broken-down bus on the quay that would take her to the Nahalal Girls School. The bus was filled not only with newcomers like herself, but with returning Palestine-born students as well. At once Hannah saw how different these girls were from the girls in Budapest.

Their nails still showed bits of earth, their hair was bleached by the sun, and their skin was dry and tanned. They wore simple white blouses and blue shorts, and they laughed loudly.

Hannah smiled at them and took her seat. She smoothed her knit dress, refolded the silk handkerchief in her pocket, and set the typewriter on her lap.

The noisy bus churned east through the Valley of Jezreel. Called the Emeq, only a few years ago this land had been nothing more than malaria-infested swampland. In the face of disease and hardship, the Zionist pioneers had worked hard to drain the swamps to create a fertile, productive valley. Orange groves, fig orchards, and wide, green fields of eggplants lay under the hot sun. Hannah stared at it all in wonder.

She saw Arab men riding donkeys, women wearing veils, and British soldiers riding in jeeps. She saw Jewish children climbing palm trees and Jewish mothers driving tractors. But most wondrous of all was the language. The shop signs, the road signs, the cries of the vendors on the streets, and the arguments of the children were in Hebrew! "Truly now I'm in a Jewish land," Hannah thought happily. At last the bus rumbled down the wide eucalyptus-shaded avenue to the school. Hannah stepped off the bus to the fragrant smell of orange orchards.

A few hours later she wrote in her dog-eared diary, "I am in Nahalal, in Eretz. I am home."

Everything Hannah saw on that first day was more beautiful than she had imagined. The low stone building of the agricultural school with its dairy, warehouse, classrooms, and synagogue were circled by lush gardens and beyond them a patchwork coverlet of crops. On the horizon stood the craggy, wooded mountains of Galilee rising into the clear blue Mediterranean sky.

Hannah was given two roommates, Miriam and Penina. To show her friendship, Hannah immediately volunteered to sweep the room. But as she swept she noticed the others girls staring at her in amusement. At last Penina took the broom from her and showed her how to use it.

"I don't even know how to sweep," Hannah thought unhappily to herself.

"Don't worry," Penina soothed. "You are like a plant that has been uprooted, that's all. You'll soon learn."

When her roommates left the room later, Hannah buried her head in the pillow and sobbed, the same way she had done many times as a child. She wanted to be a Zionist pioneer, not an upper-class Hungarian schoolgirl. She would have to change if she were ever to belong to this new life. "Dear God," Hannah prayed, "give me the strength to change."

As the weeks passed, Hannah did change. The girl who had never made her bed and had had her clothes washed by a maid had grown accustomed to hard work. Up at 5:30 in the morning, she climbed olive trees to pick the choicest olives, planted pomegranate trees, sprayed the orchards with powerful fertilizer guns, and shoveled cow manure as she waded knee-deep in mud.

As Hannah became accustomed to this new life of physical labor, she grew to love it. Helping young plants take root helped her own growth as a confident pioneer. She had already loved Palestine in Budapest. Now working its soil bound her to the land in an intense intimate relationship.

At the October corn harvest, Hannah found the work especially hard. The full-grown ears had to be wrenched from the withering stalks and piled into huge crates that were moved down the rows. The autumn sun beat down on the workers as they moved from stalk to stalk over the wide yellow acres.

Hannah worked feverishly, stopping only to wipe the sweat from her face with the corner of her scarf, all the while sounding a poem in her mind.

> Our people are working the black soil
> Their arms reap the gold sheaves,
> And now when the last ear its stalk leaves,
> Our faces glitter as with gilded oil.
> From where comes the new light and voice?
> From where the resounding song at hand?
> From where the fighting spirit and new faith?
> From you, fertile Emeq, from you, my Land.

By spring Hannah's fears of not adapting to the land had vanished. She put on plays, organized concerts, and arranged to have visiting speakers from neighboring settlements. She learned botany, chemistry, agriculture, fruit gardening, and how to care for livestock and poultry. By the summer of 1940 she had taken her place as one of the best students in the school. Because of this, she was entrusted with the care of the new modern chicken coops.

She took on this job enthusiastically, caring for the 400 chickens as if they were children. In the morning she gave them water and prepared their feed. She gathered their eggs and kept exact records of all that went on. Hannah loved the job. Cupping the tiny yellow chicks in her palms, she spoke to them encouragingly, "Grow up, little chick. Grow up and be strong!"

"You are like a mother hen yourself," some of the students teased, and Hannah would laugh in agreement.

"I *am* their mother now!"

Hannah was soon the poultry-farming expert. She dreamed of becoming an instructor, traveling from kibbutz to kibbutz to advise and organize their poultry raising.

But she had another dream, too—to teach children. Often she thought if she could combine agricultural work with teaching, her life would be happiest.

And then tucked away in her heart, Hannah held the dream of writing. Although she wrote to Mama "The hoe feels as comfortable in my hand now as the pen once did," she still yearned to write important and beautiful words.

Hannah was confused by all her dreams. There were so *many* things she wanted to do in Palestine, she felt as if she were floating on a wide sea of wishes, anchored to none of them. When she heard the clear, confident plans of the other students, she could not help wishing that she, too, could be content with a simple, singular direction.

After a concert she attended in Haifa, Hannah confessed her confusion in her diary:

There are so many things I don't understand, least of all myself. I would like to know who and what I really am but can only ask questions, not answer them. . . .

Today I listened to music. Sound after sound melts into harmony, each in itself but a delicate touch, empty, colorless, pointless, but all together—music. One tone soft, one loud, staccato or long, resonant, melodious, vibrant. What am I? How do the many tones within me sound all together? Are they harmonious?

During the summer of 1940, the tones within Hannah became more discordant. Reading the papers and listening to the radio, she grieved over Hitler's swift victories in Europe. Already most of western and eastern Europe was in his control. The Nazis now occupied Greece, Syria, and much of North Africa. They were invading Russia and planning the takeover of England and Ireland.

Hitler's dream of world domination was rapidly becoming true. So was his dream of Jewish destruction. Wherever the Nazis went, they set up detention camps for Jews, whom they would then deport back to Germany and Poland. In Dachau, Auschwitz, Treblinka, and other concentration camps, Jews met their death in gas chambers and furnaces at the rate of 10,000 a day.

In her brief moments away from her farm work and the chatter of her school friends, Hannah brooded over the murders in Europe, feeling both fearful and guilty. What would happen to George in Nazi-occupied France? Why had she left Mama alone in Budapest? Wasn't it extreme selfishness to seek her own happiness in Palestine? And, most important, what could she do to help her fellow Jews in Hungary?

To the other students and her teachers who adored her, she was bright and optimistic. They saw a smiling, energetic person whose life seemed to have direction and purpose. But the real Hannah, the Hannah not even Miriam or Penina knew, was the confused, often lonely young woman who felt very guilty that she was safe in Palestine.

Hannah's anxiety grew daily as new immigrants from Hungary told terrible stories. The Hungarians were now allied with the Nazis. They had formed a Jewish Labor Force of 150,000 men and had sent them to the front lines. These Jews were either shot by the Russians, by the Germans, or by their own Hungarian officers. Already 50,000 men had died of disease, starvation, and torture.

Hannah continued working in the fields, in the chicken coop, in class, and for the cultural committee. But she felt strange new stirrings within her. The time for her to make a difference in the world was drawing near. She had no idea yet how she would make this difference, but often, when she was alone, she heard an inner voice telling her that she was being singled out for something important.

On a clear April evening two years after her arrival in Palestine, rather than going to a party with Miriam and the others, Hannah chose to stroll alone through the farms of Nahalal. The night was filled with stars. Small lights from the homes glittered as she walked. All around in the warm night air she could hear the sounds of music, conversation, and laughter. And far, far in the distance she heard the nervous barking of dogs. Hannah, with her light Budapest skin now golden brown from the Palestine sun, walked slowly, breathing in the sweet, strong smell of the orchards. Her hair, uncurled, was brushed back from her face; her nails still held a bit of the soil with which she worked. Her dream of becoming a Zionist pioneer had come true. She should have felt happy, yet Hannah felt overwhelmed by loneliness. How strange it was, she thought. The houses of people seemed so distant to her and yet the stars seemed so very near. Later that night she described her strange feelings in her diary:

> Suddenly I was gripped by fear. Where is life leading me? Will I always go on alone in the night, looking at the sparkling stars, thinking they are close? Will I be unable to hear the songs . . . the songs and laughter around me? Will I fail

to turn off the lonely road in order to enter the little houses?

What must I choose? The weak lights filtering through the chinks in the houses, or the distant light of the stars? Worst of all, when I'm among the stars I long for the small lights, and when I find my way into one of the little houses my soul yearns for the heavenly bodies. I'm filled with discontent, hesitancy, insecurity, anxiety, lack of confidence.

Sometimes I feel I am an emissary who has been entrusted with a mission. What this mission is—is not clear to me. (After all everyone has a mission in life.) I feel I have a duty toward others, as if I were obligated to them. At times this appears to be all sheer nonsense, and I wonder why all this individual effort . . . and why particularly me?

eight-

Palestine 1941

In September 1941 Hannah graduated with honors from the Nahalal Girls School of Agriculture. She was anxious to leave, to apply her new knowledge to the world outside of school.

After graduation she and her friends, Miriam and Penina, began to visit kibbutzim all over Palestine. Many of these kibbutzim desperately needed workers and strongly urged Hannah to join. But she would not commit herself to any of them. Hannah rejected the kibbutz in the lush green valleys of the Galilee. She rejected the kibbutz with Hungarian settlers and the kibbutz founded by artists, writers, and intellectuals. She rejected the kibbutz with the fine tractors and chicken coops. Hannah rejected everything that suggested ease, familiarity, and comfort. "I don't want anything ready-made," she told her diary. Hannah wanted more than just to belong to a kibbutz. She wanted to begin one.

In October, Hannah visited a group of people in the ancient Roman seaport of Caesarea. Here, alongside the Mediterranean, the group planned to build a kibbutz. S'dot Yam they would call it—"Fields of the Sea"—because they would earn their living from both fishing and agriculture. Hannah liked the group. They were daring, energetic, and poor. All they had was a plot of dry land, a few boats, some fishing nets, and round canvas tents. But the pioneers at S'dot Yam had dreams, beautiful dreams of a self-sufficient community rising from the crumbled ruins of the Roman city. Hannah shared their vision.

In December, Hannah decided to join S'dot Yam. Right away she wanted to prove to the other members that she would fit in. She gathered up her silk dresses, pretty scarves, and warm coats she had brought to Palestine two years earlier. These clothes were now alien "Diaspora" clothes to her. She put them in the kibbutz storeroom. Now she would be a true pioneer.

But being a true pioneer was hard, hard work. Hannah and Penina, who had also joined S'dot Yam, lived together in a small tent which they frequently had to set up after the sea winds blew it down. Though the tents were cramped, dim, and drafty, Hannah tried to make hers cheerful. She pasted magazine pictures to the rickety orange crates that held her belongings, and she arranged the wild purple cyclamen she gathered from the fields into little jars beside their cots.

Despite her attempts to civilize her life at S'dot Yam, she soon saw the work was difficult and tedious.

"Today I washed 150 pairs of socks. I thought I'd go mad," she confided to her diary.

For eight and a half hours each day Hannah stood outside over a large tin tub and washed clothes in icy cold sea water. The water nearly froze her fingers, and her legs ached from the constant standing.

When night came, Hannah visited nearby settlements to work with children in the neighboring Zionist youth groups. She organized camps for them, told them stories of brave Jewish heroes and heroines in history, and taught them to make little toys and gifts. Working with the children calmed Hannah's restless soul and erased the drudgery of her day's work.

A year passed, and Hannah became known for her clever ideas and strong views. She was liked and admired by the others, for she had proved that no work was too hard or unpleasant for her. She had scrubbed chicken coops, cleaned latrines, mended fishing nets, cooked, and had even hired herself out as a cleaning woman in the surrounding villages. "Hannah is strong as a man," the others said. "If you want something done, get Hannah."

To show their trust in her, the kibbutz members elected her supply officer in charge of all tools and communal property of the kibbutz. But even though Hannah was flattered, she felt the task was not challenging enough for her.

Now she had the admiration of the whole kibbutz, several boyfriends, and a close friendship with Penina. Yet she was still lonely. To her diary she confessed:

> I live in a world of my own making, without any contact with the outside world. I live here like a drop of oil on water, sometimes afloat, sometimes submerged, but always remaining apart, never mixing with another drop.

On the Sabbath, Hannah especially loved to be alone. On these days of no work, she would often stroll along the seacoast, stopping on the way to pick wildflowers. Taking her diary with her, she could at last have time to think and write.

Sitting on a rock looking over the vast blue sea, Hannah was comforted. The rhythm of the waves calmed her troubled mind and made her feel not as lonely.

> You are not alone. Here is your sea.
> The sand, the shore, the sea, the waves,
> The dreams, the hopes that brought you here.

They waited for your coming. They stayed:
The sand, the shore, the sea, the waves.
They knew: the black night would bring you here.

And the myriad eyes in the sky
Wink into your two from on high
Stealing from the endless sea—a tear.

In the spring of 1942 the workers of S'dot Yam had moved to permanent surroundings. Now Hannah had her own tiny room with a skinny bed, a small table, and a metal closet for clothes.

The kibbutz members had plowed, fertilized, and watered their fields, and the land lay ready for the planting of corn, eggplants, and tomatoes.

Hannah planted crops during the day. At night, while the

others slept, she strained her eyes in the dim light of a kerosene lamp to read letters from home, from Evi and from Mama.

"I'm well, only my hair has turned gray," Mama wrote. The words frightened Hannah. The Third Anti-Jewish Bill passed that fall was in full effect. All relationships between Jews and non-Jews were strictly forbidden. The worst accusation now was to label someone a Jew. When an anonymous note to Horthy claimed that Prime Minister Teleki's grandmother was Jewish, Teleki committed suicide. László Bardossy succeeded Teleki. Bardossy was completely sympathetic with Nazi anti-Jewish ravings. Because of Bardossy, the Jews in Hungary feared for their lives more than ever. Their fate was sealed. Hitler was furious that only in Hungary were the majority of Jews still alive. He demanded that Bardossy

- send the 800,000 Jews of Hungary to be "resettled" by the Germans
- make the Jews wear the yellow Star of David armband
- confiscate all money, land, and belongings of Jews

"I must get Mama out of Hungary!" Hannah told herself.

She wrote to her mother, urging her to come to Palestine, and tried desperately to get her a visa. Hannah's efforts were useless. The British had severely restricted Jewish emigration to Palestine with their White Paper of 1939. Even in the face of mass protests and pleas, they remained stubborn. The White Paper let only 75,000 Jews enter Palestine. Hannah knew this left millions more to die.

Many Palestinian Jews worked hard to smuggle in Jews from Europe. They bought and borrowed ships and loaded them with exhausted Jews at various ports. Under cover of darkness, they let the boats slip silently into the ports and smuggled the refugees ashore. The work was dangerous. If caught, the boats were turned back at once. Many boats were rickety, and some sank before reaching shore.

In the summer of 1942, while Hannah agonized over her

mother and her own inability to help, she read a book by the Hebrew novelist Hazaz. The book, *Broken Grindstones*, had a sentence in it that moved her deeply: "All the darkness can't extinguish a single candle; yet one candle can illuminate all the darkness."

Hannah could not rid her mind of this image. "Could I," she wondered, "really do something to help those who are suffering in Europe?"

The question possessed her, giving her no rest. Whatever she did, fishing in the sea or working with her youth group, her mind burned with the question. Then, in January 1943, the answer came to her. She wrote in her diary:

> I've had a shattering week. I was suddenly struck by the idea of going to Hungary. I feel I must be there during these days in order to help organize youth emigration and also to get my mother out. Although I'm quite aware how absurd the idea is, it still seems feasible and necessary to me, so I'll get to work on it and carry it through.

Hannah did not let the idea go. She traveled to Tel Aviv to enlist in the Haganah, the Jewish Palestinian defense unit of the British army. She was told to wait. She would be notified when and if she was accepted.

Hannah could no longer sleep. She tossed from side to side, staring into the darkness, filling it with wild images. She imagined how she would get back to Hungary, how she would contact her mother, what she would say to the Jews of Budapest, even how she would disguise herself.

> I imagine various situations and sometimes think about leaving the Land ... leaving the freedom.... I would like to inhale enough fresh air so as to be able to breathe it even in the Diaspora's stifling atmosphere, and to spread it all around me for those who do not know what real freedom is.

Month after month Hannah waited to be called. She was

confident and ready when, at last, in December 1943 she was given word that she had been accepted into the Haganah. She would need to train at Kibbutz Ramat Hakovesh, near Tel Aviv, with the British army before going to Cairo, Egypt, for a dangerous secret mission.

Hannah was ecstatic.

> I see the hand of destiny in this just as I did at the time of my Aliyah. . . . Now I again sense the excitement of something important and vital ahead.

Just before she left, Hannah wrote to George in France, urging him to try to get to Palestine and explaining her own reasons for joining the army.

"Darling George, there are events without which one's life becomes unimportant, a worthless toy; and there are times when one is commanded to do something, even at the price of one's life."

During her training Hannah left her diary behind at S'dot Yam. But on the eleventh of January 1944, Hannah returned to S'dot Yam to pack her belongings. On that day she wrote her final diary entry:

> This week I leave for Egypt. I am a soldier. . . . I want to believe that what I've done and will do are right. Time will tell the rest.

The afternoon before Hannah left for Egypt, she took a last walk down to the sea. The gray water splashed wildly on the rocks while white seagulls skimmed and fluttered over the water like handkerchiefs. Hannah looked out to the horizon where the gray sea met the gray sky in one soft, silver sunset. She was giving up everything. This beautiful sea, her work in the Land, and S'dot Yam. Although she had often felt lonely here, S'dot Yam was her home ... her only home. She was leaving it, for now she was at a crossroads in her life. Leaving the life she loved to help the people she loved.

Perhaps one day this terrible war will end, she thought. Then Jews from all over Europe will come to Eretz to build our land. "God," Hannah prayed, "let me return to help them."

It began to rain as Hannah walked back from the sea to the kibbutz. She packed her father's books, her poems, and the many notebooks of her diary into her suitcase. She locked it, then carried the heavy load over to the kibbutz secretary. She asked the kibbutz for two favors: to take care of her mother should she arrive in her absence, and to keep the suitcase until she returned.

The next morning, a cold winter's wind blew the sand from the coast across the bare fields. Hannah, dressed in the blue-gray uniform of the British air force, left S'dot Yam. Her diary and her life in the Land had ended.

nine-

Egypt 1944

The five young people laughed and talked wildly as the car sped southward toward Egypt. Hannah was at the wheel, and in the vast, bleak desert she was enjoying the freedom to race across the sands, hurling herself and the others forward to their intelligence training in Cairo.

"Watch out! You're going too fast!" Yoel cried out, covering his eyes in terror as a car raced toward them.

Hannah shook her brown hair back over her shoulders and laughed, "Don't be afraid, I'm a very careful driver—just a little fast."

Everyone laughed. Even though there were two British military drivers in the car, Hannah had persuaded them to let her drive. She had never been behind the wheel before, and her inexperience, combined with her speed, at first terrified her passengers. But after a while, they realized that this warm, energetic Hungarian girl knew exactly what she was doing.

The group broke into song. Their Hebrew words floated out into the parched desert as the car flew past sand-colored Arab villages and lonely camel caravans. Hannah and the four

men—Yoel Palgi, Ben Ephraim, Yohen Rosen, and Abba Ber-
dichev—were friends and fellow missionaries. They were five
of the thirty-two men and women selected by the Haganah
and the British army for a dangerous mission. In a few days,
dressed in British air force uniforms, they would be parachuted into Hungary. Their mission would be to open escape
routes for downed British airmen. The excitement of the im-
pending drop made them close, nervous, emotional friends.
They had just finished a grueling month of basic training and
parachuting at Ramat Hakovesh and were now destined for
a top-secret suicide mission, yet they joked as if on a school
outing.

"I'll tell you what we'll do," Yoel shouted over the low roar
of the car's engine. "When the war is over and we're big
heroes, we'll get the British air force to parachute each of us
into our own kibbutz. Won't that be a true hero's return!"

Everyone laughed and agreed it was the only proper way
for a hero to return. They jostled each other and sang while
Hannah translated the joke for the benefit of the British drivers.

Hannah felt good about her decision to join the Haganah.
Although the British were concerned only with the safety of
their pilots, Hannah knew that once she was back in Hungary
she would find the way to help the Jews. She would open up
escape routes, give courage to the Resistance fighters, and
warn the Jews of Hitler's evil plans. "I will make a difference
in the world!" Hannah thought.

She was certain she would succeed. In basic training she
had done amazingly well. She had learned judo, the use of
various knives, and how to use the "kapop," the little club
the shepherds carried. And though she dreaded the thought
of using them, she could fire captured German arms, over-
coming her fright at their load noise and kickback. Stens,
German Schmeissers, and Colt .45s were as familiar to her
now as hoes, rakes, and shovels.

Most important, she had conquered her paralyzing fear of

parachuting. At her maiden jump, when she stood weak-kneed and dry-mouthed at the open door, she thought surely she would faint. But somehow she had jumped. Her parachute had opened, and she had fallen thousands of feet toward Palestine.

Hannah drove confidently through the Sinai desert, feeling strong and eager for the next challenge.

In Cairo, Hannah and the others faced an awful disappointment. They would not, the British said, be parachuted into Hungary. It was far too dangerous, for now the Nazis were planning a full-scale invasion of that country. Instead, they would be dropped into neighboring Yugoslavia, where they would locate downed British pilots.

Hannah was furious. Her dream was to save Hungarian Jews, not wander around the forests of Yugoslavia! The four boys accepted this news. Only Hannah argued with the British over their decision. "We have no time to wait!" she said. "It is now, *now,* that Hungary is almost in Nazi hands that we are most needed there!"

The British were firm. Their real interest was not in saving the 1 million Jews trapped in Hungary. They wanted to help the Resistance fighters and their own pilots in Yugoslavia.

Hannah poured out her frustration to Yoel. He was her closest friend. In Tel Aviv, after their training, they had shared wonderful conversations and had laughed together. They had gone to movies, plays, and restaurants. Hannah sometimes thought that Yoel was falling in love with her. Now she told him of her unhappiness at not being able to get to Hungary.

"You are very stubborn," Yoel replied. "But we must wait. We can't act on our own but must follow British orders. Hannah, you must resign yourself to that. We will get our chance to help the Jews if we are patient. Arguing all day with the British won't help! Remember, Hannah," Yoel said gently, "sometimes you are wrong."

Hannah knew Yoel talked sense. She knew she was passionate and impatient. He was level-headed and calm. "I must learn to be patient," she told herself. "But it is so hard!"

Weeks passed in Cairo, and Hannah completed her intelligence training. Now she was confident she could create and decipher codes. If she were captured, she could easily mislead the enemy.

In March, the British decided to fly Hannah and three men—Reuven Dafne, Abba Birchner, and Peretz Goldstein—to Italy. Italy had been liberated by the British army and was now a safe place for the four to prepare for their jump into Yugoslavia. Yoel would join them with a second group two weeks later.

Hannah had been given permission to cross into Hungary soon after they landed in Yugoslavia. She was getting closer and closer to her final goal.

At the Brindisi airport, in southeastern Italy, the British airmen working in the parachute storeroom looked in amazement at the slender woman in the blue-gray British uniform. At first, some of them thought it was a joke. "She must be someone's wife coming to say good-by," they reasoned. But later, when they saw the same pretty woman in a bulky paratrooper outfit, they were stunned. "What kind of woman is this?" One by one, each man wished her well and shook her hand.

In the last hours before the plane took off the group was tense. Their concealed knives and guns hung heavy beneath their clothes. Reuven's leg was strapped with an incendiary bomb. Hannah's blouse concealed the radio transmitter to communicate with Allied pilots. The responsibility and danger of their mission had at last sobered their high spirits.

Abba sat in a corner of the hangar writing endless letters to his family. Reuven, who had just been told his family had been sent to the Dachau concentration camp, sat in another corner in despair. For hours Hannah tried to comfort him, to lift up his hopes. "Soon the war will be over and your family will be free," she told Reuven. He wanted desperately to believe her, but he feared he would never see his family again.

In these sad, tense hours Hannah wrote letters, too. She wrote to her mother, being careful not to reveal anything of the secret mission. Then she wrote to S'dot Yam, urging them all to continue the struggle of creating a land for the Jews. "We are all advancing toward the same goal," she told them. "I will be thinking of you a great deal. That's what gives me strength."

Then at midnight, in the cold, dim light of the airport hangar, while the others wrote and talked around her, Hannah began to work on a poem.

> We gathered flowers in the fields and mountains
> We breathed the fresh winds of spring
> We were drenched with the warmth of the sun's rays
> In our Homeland, in our beloved home.
>
> We go out to our brothers in exile
> To the suffering of winter, to frost in the night.
> Our hearts will bring tidings of springtime
> Our lips sing the song of light.

With a tremendous roar, the propellers of the cargo plane were started up. Hannah quickly put the poem in her pocket to work on later. She lifted the heavy radio equipment onto her shoulders, checked to see her gun was in place, and entered the black cargo hold of the plane.

ten-

Yugoslavia 1944

The jump into Yugoslavia was successful. Although Hannah's light body was blown off course, she caught up with the others a few hours later in the forest of Slovenia, northern Yugoslavia. The Jewish paratroopers were greeted immediately by Resistance fighters wearing the red star of Communism on their caps. They had been fighting the Nazis for a month. Their clothes were in tatters, and, though snow covered the ground, they went barefoot. The sight of the Jewish youths in British uniforms cheered the Resistance fighters, and they gave a whistle signal for others in the hills to join them. Soon Hannah, Peretz, Abba, and Reuven were surrounded by Resistance fighters grinning at each other like school children. "Death to the fascists! Freedom to the people!" the Resistance fighters cheered.

Hannah cheered with them. Now her work would begin. "In a few days," she thought, "I will be in Hungary—perhaps in Budapest with Mama."

But Hannah's dream was not to be. Sitting in the Resistance fighters' forest headquarters on March 18, Hannah and Reuven were the first to hear the terrible news—the Nazis had marched into Budapest. All of Hungary was in Nazi hands.

Hannah was crushed. She had planned to enter Hungary disguised as a Jewish refugee, but now that was impossible.

Hannah had convinced herself that she could be strong, objective, soldierly. But the heartbreak was too much, and she wept bitterly.

Reuven tried to comfort her. He had often heard her speak of her mother in Budapest, and now he said the encouraging words she had given him in Brindisi—that the war would end soon.

"What will happen to all of them, the million Jews in Hungary?" she sobbed. "They're in German hands now. And we're sitting here—just sitting!"

From the moment Hannah heard the terrible news about Hungary, she could not rest. She *would* get to Hungary, she told herself. She *must* get to Hungary now. "God," she prayed, "show me the way."

In the meantime, the area of Yugoslavia they were in had also just been taken over by the Nazis. If they were to continue their underground activities, they would have to make their way to the next province, Croatia, where the Resistance still had control. Hannah and the others started the long trek to Croatia. In the melting winter, they roamed the forests and crossed high mountains, meeting up with other freedom fighters and constantly looking out for Nazis.

Wherever they went, people stared at Hannah. Often the Resistance fighters in a village traveled expressly to see her. They had heard tales of a lovely young woman who had dropped into their country to help them fight the Nazis. Now they wanted to see this remarkable legend.

One evening Hannah and the others were invited to a local festival. Men and women in uniforms crowded the town hall, laughing and talking loudly. As Hannah and the other para-

troopers entered the hall, they were cheered wildly as representatives of the British Empire. Most Resistance fighters had no idea they were Jewish. When Hannah and the others spoke Hebrew, they were told it was Welsh. Hannah was sad that they could not let their true identities be known, but she knew many members of the Resistance were anti-Semitic. It was safer to be thought of as British soldiers.

At the festival, a British colonel suddenly asked Hannah to come forward and speak. With Reuven translating her Hebrew into Croatian, Hannah spoke fervently of the nobility of their work and the sure victory they would have over the Nazis. After each sentence, the Resistance fighters clapped and cheered.

After her speech, Hannah was surprised to see the Resistance fighters join hands with her and dance. With rifles strapped to their backs and grenades looped to their belts, the group danced for hours, forgetting for a brief time that death and destruction surrounded them.

The journey to Croatia was slow and dangerous. Hannah slogged through two hundred miles of Nazi-held territory, along the path of the railroad which ran from Vienna to Belgrade. This route was especially guarded. All along it stood pillboxes, concrete structures in which Nazis crouched with machine guns to shoot at any suspected enemy. As they traveled, they received information from the Yugoslav Resistance as to the Nazis' activities. This information Hannah imparted by radio transmitter to the British.

They trudged at night through damp forests and swamps and across rivers. Often they did not sleep for more than an hour or two a night and ate only every other day, yet they never stopped. They were determined to travel as quickly as possible.

One night the group found itself in a village near the border—enemy territory. Suddenly, the village resounded with a burst of gunfire. The Nazis were attacking! Immediately, the Resistance fighters fled, escaping wherever they could. The villagers ran screaming through the streets, hiding behind rocks or sliding down the hillsides into a narrow ravine.

Hannah and Reuven began to run. They were surrounded by the enemy. Where—where could they go! They found themselves at a cliff overlooking a valley. Quickly, they tied one end of a rope to a tree and shinnied down the rope to the bottom. Now they were in an open valley, completely exposed to the bullets the Nazis were firing from the hills above.

Hannah's heart beat so fast she thought she would collapse. But she kept on running and stumbling, running and stumbling, thinking only of survival. As she ran, villagers fleeing into the same valley from another route stumbled beside her. Old men drove cattle before them, beating them mercilessly to hurry. Women carried their crying children as well as whatever belongings they could run with: soup pots, pillows, jewelry boxes. The screams of the women and the cries of the children echoed in Hannah's ears, interrupted only by the staccato cracks of guns being fired.

Destruction surrounded them. Hannah tripped over bodies as she ran, trying to keep up with Reuven, running, trying to reach the forest.

Gasping for breath, Hannah and Reuven came at last to the forest, where they dropped to the ground, exhausted but safe.

Hours passed while Reuven and Hannah lay silently in the bushes, holding their pistols and looking around. They could hear the fire of machine guns. Then suddenly, through the bushes, Hannah saw a group of German soldiers directly in front of them. To her horror, Hannah saw Reuven lift his pistol and take aim. His finger tightened on the trigger.

"Stop it! Don't shoot!" Hannah whispered. Reuven looked at her. She said nothing more, but her eyes spoke to him. "We are not here to kill the enemy. We are here to rescue our people."

Hannah and Reuven stayed in the forest that night, and the next day they trudged on toward Croatia. Night after night they arrived in unknown villages, relying on the hospitality of members of the Resistance. As representatives of the British air force, they not only relayed important military information to the Resistance but gave encouragement and hope as well.

One night, in a small village, Reuven met a woman who had been his childhood friend. She, a Jew, was surprised and delighted to see Jews from Palestine. Hannah and Reuven talked excitedly about the beauty of Palestine, and the woman, in turn, told them about the lives of the Jews in Europe.

Her description of Jewish life in Hungary was far worse than anything Hannah had imagined. Only a few weeks ago, the woman said, Jews in Hungary had to register their property, and all Jewish-owned shops, offices, and factories were closed. The Nazis confiscated all Jewish money. Next, they would seize Jewish property. Jews could not buy their ration of meat, butter, rice, and eggs. They were forbidden to listen to the radio, to make telephone calls, or to use public transport. Jews could not ride bikes or sit in a park or leave home without permission, and then only to shop. "Even looking out the window is forbidden," the woman told them. "Jews must not look into the street."

"But what will happen?" Hannah cried. "What will happen to the Jews?"

"Don't you know?" the woman said impatiently. "They are being told to assemble in 'star houses,' special apartments where Jews are crowded before they are shipped to their deaths in the concentration camps in Germany and Poland. Already thousands of children have been sent."

Hannah was shaken. The woman's words told her she needed to be totally single-minded and self-sacrificing. More than ever, she felt on fire with the passion of her mission. A few days later, in the town of Sardice, Hannah put her passion into a poem.

Blessed is the match consumed
  in kindling flame.
Blessed is the flame that burns
  in the secret fastness of the heart.
Blessed is the heart with strength to stop
  its beating for honor's sake.
Blessed is the match consumed
  in kindling flame.

Hannah's obsession with saving Jews changed her. By the time Yoel joined her group in Sardice, she was not the same high-spirited, cheerful girl he had known in Tel Aviv and Cairo. Hannah had grown apart from everyone. She no longer chatted, only complained. She conveyed information to the Resistance with her radio, but that alone would not save Jews. "I have nothing *specific* to do!" Hannah said many times. She was angry that Yoel and Reuven had clear jobs to do. Both had to open up escape routes from Hungary to Yugoslavia and create maps for the Resistance which showed exactly which bits of land were free of Nazis. Frustrated by her inability to help the Jews directly, Hannah was wrapped in her own fear and loneliness. In the stables of the peasants where they often stayed at night, Hannah did not enter the conversations but remained apart, quiet and brooding. Gone was her smile and dewey-eyed hope. She had important work to do, and she was not doing it. The thought made her miserable.

One night she and Yoel were sitting around a bonfire in an open field. They were waiting with other Resistance fighters for a British plane to drop supplies. The group sang Resistance songs, but Hannah could not join in. Suddenly she got up and asked Yoel to walk with her. As they walked in the black, still night Hannah confessed her unhappiness and told him of her plan.

"I want to enter Hungary, no matter what," she said. "It's better to die and free our conscience than to return with the knowledge that we didn't even try."

"It's not up to you," Yoel argued. "We are under British authority—we cannot mutiny."

"But for *me*," Hannah said passionately, "this is not a question that can be decided by authority!"

All night, while the Resistance fighters sang, Yoel tried to reason with Hannah. Over and over again he told her it was dangerous to enter Hungary now and very unlikely that she, one Jewish woman, could save anyone.

But Hannah countered his logic with logic all her own: "Even if the chances of our success are small, we must go. If we don't for fear of our lives, a million Jews will surely be killed."

Yoel gave up. Hannah was passionate, persuasive, and maybe even right. Suddenly he took her hand into his own. "We will go," he said. "We will go to Hungary and free our people!"

Hannah's face lit up. "We will," she answered smiling, "and one day, Yoel, thousands of Jewish Resistance fighters will be sitting around campfires like this, singing songs of Eretz. The forest of Europe will echo with the songs of Jewish freedom fighters."

The next day, Hannah and Yoel set out for Hungary. So as not to arouse suspicion, they decided to walk on separate routes—Hannah from the east, Yoel from the north. If all went well, they would meet in Budapest the following week. Before they parted, Hannah and Yoel hugged each other in farewell. "Meet me at the Great Synagogue on Dohány Street after the Sabbath service next Friday," Hannah said. "And if Jewish services are no longer allowed there, meet me in front of the cathedral."

Hannah gave Yoel her "thumbs up" sign of victory. Yoel gave her "thumbs up" back. Then he turned and set off for the border.

The hour before Hannah was to leave for the border, Reuven Dafne tried to dissuade her from such a foolish, dangerous idea. At the farm of Resistance fighters, they strolled after supper in an apple orchard. Reuven told her how very risky it was to cross into Hungary. "It's a crazy idea," he said, "and too dangerous!"

But Hannah would not be swayed by his words. When at last he realized her mind was made up, he offered to accompany her to the border. Hannah refused. "I don't see the point of both of us risking our lives."

Minutes before she left, Hannah created a dream for all the paratroopers: "When we get back to Eretz, we'll rent a big bus and travel from kibbutz to kibbutz, telling stories and celebrating. We'll tell them everything that happened . . . and make up a few tall tales too!"

Reuven could not join in her dream. He was overwhelmed with sadness. Suddenly, Hannah took from her pocket a wrinkled scrap of paper with the poem she had written in Sardice. "If I don't return, Reuven, give this to our people."

Reuven said nothing. He shook her hand and watched her walk away from him. At the bend in the road, she stopped and waved good-by.

Suddenly, his sadness turned to anger. Why should a young, inexperienced Jewish woman be allowed to enter Nazi territory alone? He feared for this impulsive Hannah, who had become his friend. Though he had spent hours trying to dissuade her from leaving, she had ignored his advice. Now she was gone. Without even glancing at it, Reuven crumpled the paper and threw it into the bushes.

eleven-

Hungary 1944

The Hungarian Regal Government shall cleanse the
country of Jews within a short time. I am ordering the
cleansing to take place by regions, resulting in the de-
livery of all Jews in concentration camps, regardless of
their sex or age. . . . The captives shall be transported by
train.

—Confidential Decree of the Department of the Interior with
Respect to Deporting Jews to Concentration Camps, April 7, 1944

By the time Hannah crossed the border into Hungary, half of
Hungary's Jews had already been murdered. From the villages
and farms they were herded into barbed-wire enclosures
without food or water. Often they were so crowded they were
forced to sleep standing up. From these deportation centers,
the Jews were jammed into cattle cars of freight trains heading for the concentration camps of Auschwitz, Dachau, and
Treblinka. Aided by the Hungarian Arrow Cross, the Germans
were able to round up Jews peacefully. From those Jews who
disappeared came a flood of postcards to those who remained. "Have arrived . . . I am well." Often the postcards
were written at the very gates of the concentration camps.

The letters, of course, were fake, their authors forced at gunpoint to write the comforting words that would disarm their relatives.

The ploy worked. Most Jews in Hungary still did not understand that the Nazis had only one plan for them—death.

In Budapest the Jews were not yet deported. But every day thousands of Jews were moved into Yellow Star Houses. These buildings, emblazoned with a yellow Star of David, held the Jews until the Nazis could send them to concentration camps.

On the same day that Hannah smuggled herself across the border to Hungary, her mother was making a painful decision. Like all Jews in Budapest, Catherine had been ordered to move into a Yellow Star House. But an elderly Jewish couple next door had persuaded her to flee to Romania with them disguised as Christians. From Romania, they told her, it was easy to get to Palestine. Catherine Szenes doubted the safety of such a trip, but even the smallest chance to escape—the smallest chance to see Hannah again—was a strong temptation.

Catherine had lost her home. Since Jews were not allowed to own property, her good Christian friend, actress Margit Dayka, registered the house in her name and lived in it with her. Margit promised Catherine to guard the house well until the war's end.

Catherine told Margit of her plans and prepared for her escape. As she packed, she agonized over those she would leave behind in Hungary. Her sister's family in Dombóvár had already been deported—but to where? She had not heard from them in months.

What Catherine did not know was that all those in Dombóvár, including her niece, Hannah's beloved cousin Evi, had already been killed in Auschwitz.

Hannah's entry into Hungary was easier than she had expected. With the help of two members of the Jewish underground, Kallos and Fleishman, and Jacques Tissandier, a Christian French Resistance fighter, Hannah walked across the frontier easily. But once inside Hungary, the four wandered around aimlessly for hours. They were trying to get to Budapest, but their map- and compass-reading skills were not good. At last the group discovered the river Dráva.

Standing in front of the icy, swift-flowing river, Jacques said, "If we are ever to reach Budapest, we've got to cross the river. But you, Hannah, must give up the radio transmitter. It's too heavy to swim with, and, besides, if the Germans find us with it, they'll think we're spies."

Jacques knew what he was talking about. He had already escaped from the Germans seven times. But Hannah would not listen. His words only made her mind race with worries. How could she relay messages to the British without it? She had not come this far to give up the precious transmitter now.

"I won't give it up," she said. "We can take it apart and carry the parts separately across the river. This will make the swimming easier."

Jacques did not like the idea, but the two days he had been with this young woman told him she was stubborn and would have her way. He helped her take apart the bulky radio transmitter. Then the three men and Hannah, holding a piece of transmitter under each arm, crossed the swirling water.

They crossed three more rivers during the night and at dawn reached the edge of a small town. Kallos thought the town was Mureska Subatica, on the road to Budapest. To be sure, he entered the village with Fleishman, while Hannah and Jacques hid in the reeds by the water. Hannah waited there, shivering with cold. When Kallos and Fleishman did not return after three hours, Hannah grew frightened. As she tried to stop the horrible images that raced through her mind, she suddenly heard a loud stomping and rustling in the reeds. Soldiers were looking for them!

"Come!" Jacques whispered. "Crawl!" For the next hour

Hannah and Jacques crawled on their stomachs through the thick reeds to a nearby forest. There the two hastily buried the transmitter and their pistols. As they dug desperately into the ground with their bare hands, they heard the sound of footsteps and shouting.

They had been followed! In a moment they would be surrounded by hundreds of soldiers. Hannah and Jacques threw themselves into each other's arms, kissing and hugging passionately, so that if discovered they would look no more guilty than a pair of lovers.

In less than a minute they were found. The Hungarian police officer heading the search looked them up and down. One dark-haired girl in slacks, dirty and disheveled, and one young man, scruffy and wrinkled.

The officer signaled his partner to handcuff the pair. "You *look* innocent enough," he said, "but I will have to take you in for questioning." Smiling slyly at Hannah, he added, "If you are innocent, in an hour you can get back to your love-making."

Hannah went numb with fear. She was glad they had buried the transmitter. Perhaps if they could stay calm and lie well, they would be released. But, arriving at police headquarters in the town, Hannah lost all hope. There, slumped in a chair, sat Fleishman, his face bloody and bruised from a recent beating. Nearby on a table lay Kallos—dead.

"We found earphones to a radio transmitter in his pocket," said the police commandant, pointing to the corpse. "One of you had a transmitter, and we will find it, too."

For two days Hannah was beaten. The soldiers punched her face repeatedly, knocking out her front tooth. Although she slipped in and out of consciousness and was in excruciating pain, she still would not tell them where the radio transmitter was.

She did not have to. The Hungarian and German soldiers searched every inch of land for miles. They destroyed all the corn crops of the village until, at last, they found the trans-

mitter. Hannah's guilt was proven—she was pronounced an enemy of Hungary. "You are a spy, a traitor. You will be transported to the Miklós Horthy military prison in Budapest," the Hungarian commandant said.

The train speeding to Budapest passed the calm, blue waters of Lake Balaton. Sailboats skimmed the lake, and the spring sun shone on the bathers relaxing on its shores. Hannah looked at the scene from the train window but saw nothing. Handcuffed, exhausted, aching from her beatings, she thought of only one thing—her failure. Her mission to help Hungary's Jews had ended before it even began. Now she would be forced to betray the others, to give away the code to the radio transmitter. And once the Nazis had this, they could give false information to the British. Hannah looked down at her battered little red book lying beside her. "How stupid they are," Hannah thought. This book of French poetry they had allowed her to take along had the code cleverly concealed within it. Hannah waited until she was sure the guard was distracted by the bathers outside the window. Then she let the book fall to the floor and kicked it under the seat. The book would be left on the train, and she would never be able to reveal the code.

But Hannah had other information important to the Nazis, and, as the train rattled monotonously toward Budapest, she doubted she could stand any more torture. Perhaps in her agony she would reveal something that would endanger the lives of the other paratroopers.

The guard rose to go to the bathroom. Hannah moved quickly. With the limited movement of her locked hands, she struggled to open the heavy door of the train. The wind blew into her face, and when she looked down it seemed the land was racing backward. Now she would do it. Now she would throw herself out the train and end her life.

"You are state property!" A rough hand grabbed her shoulder and pulled her back from the open door. The guard's angry face loomed over her. Hannah thought in his fury he would beat her, but he threw her down into the seat. "You are state property!" he repeated. "We will do away with you when we no longer need you!"

Arriving at the military prison in the Budapest she had once loved, Hannah was stripped naked, bound in chains, and beaten. For days the Hungarian police whipped her and pulled out handfuls of hair.

"Tell us your name!" they shouted at her over and over again, but Hannah would reveal only her false name—Maria. They did not believe her. "Tell us your name! *Tell us your name!*"

They knocked out a tooth and beat her steadily for three hours, but still Hannah only mumbled, "I am Maria."

After several days Hannah was brought before Sergeant Rosja, the chief prison inspector. In his dusty office overlooking the grim prison yard, Hannah was put in a chair to face her inquisitor. Sergeant Rosja lit a cigarette, then pressed the button to start the little tape recorder on his desk.

"You are a Hungarian—we are sure of that," he said. "Your accent betrays your birth. They tell me that in Sombotje, at the border, you lied to the Gestapo. But you will not lie to me. Anyway, I already know the truth—you are a traitor to your own land. Your radio transmitter was used to help British pilots bomb Hungarian cities."

Hannah could not talk with her swollen, bloody mouth, but she mumbled what she had repeated throughout her torture, "I am a British prisoner of war and request to be treated as such." She stared bravely at Rosja all the while.

"Perhaps this will make you talk," Rosja said. "Your fellow spy, Jacques, is in the next room. If you don't tell us your real name, we will kill him—now."

Hannah said nothing. Rosja continued, "All I need to do is press this button on my desk, and the execution will be carried out. Now, are you going to tell me your name?"

Hannah remained silent, staring at Rosja, but in her heart she had lost all hope. She knew full well this cruel man would kill Jacques if she did not reveal her identity. But if she told her name, then she would be putting her mother in danger. They would use Mama's life to further blackmail her. For a moment, Hannah's stoic face betrayed her torment. Rosja grinned and lowered his finger over the button.

The words spilled out of her. "My name is Hannah Szenes."

twelve-

The warm air of the Budapest summer morning did not penetrate the high brick wall of the military prison. Hannah's cell was cold. Dust lay on the cracked cement floor, and the walls smelled of mildew. Hannah lay on the thin, dirty cot and shivered. She had shivered all night, and now her teeth chattered, too. Her thin prison dress was inadequate, so in the morning she had to move around to get warm. Around and around her tiny cell she walked, around and around like a caged animal. This time Hannah tried to vary the pace and the route. Two long strides from cot to wall, then eight small steps from cell door to back wall. Around and around—six short steps and two long strides. Four long strides and three short steps. Around and around and around.

"C'mon, hurry up!" Four guards suddenly appeared at her cell door. They pulled her out of her cell and marched her down the dark corridor to Rosja's office. Hannah knew the routine by now. She would be interrogated, beaten, then interrogated again. On entering the familiar room, Hannah suddenly felt her knees give way beneath her. The guards pushed her forward. There, in front of her, stood a frail, gray-haired woman with a yellow Star of David sewn to her coat.

"Mama!" Hannah screamed, flinging herself wildly at the bewildered woman. "Mama, forgive me!"

Mama caressed Hannah's hair but said nothing.

"Speak to her!" Rosja shouted. "Use your maternal influence to convince her she'd better tell us everything or you'll never see each other again!"

Rosja and the four guards left, leaving a detective behind to keep an eye on the two women. He ordered Hannah and her mother to sit opposite each other on two wooden chairs. For a few moments, the mother and the daughter, who had not seen each other in five years, were so filled with emotion they could not talk. At last, Hannah's mother said, "I don't know why you are here in Budapest—in Hungary. I thought you were safe in Palestine. Was it because of me, Aniko, to save me, that you came back to Hungary?"

"No, Mama, no! Don't blame yourself. I didn't come back only for you." Hannah looked at Mama through her tears. Five years had passed since she had waved good-by to Mama through the steamy train window on a Rosh Hashanah eve. Now she could not even hug her mother, let alone tell her why she had come back.

Sensing the wisdom of her daughter's silence, Mama reached out to caress Hannah's hair. The once curly, soft locks were now tangled into matted knots and filthy with sweat and caked blood. Hannah's hands were as dry as paper and full of open cuts. And her face . . .

"Of course, your tooth was knocked out here," Mama said gently.

"No, not at all," Hannah lied as Mama stroked the bruises and welts on her swollen cheeks. Mama leaned over to kiss Hannah's black eyes, when the door was flung open.

"Whispering is not allowed here!" Rosja shouted. "Go home, Mrs. Szenes. We'll call you if we need you, but don't speak a word of what you've seen here to anyone!"

Hannah did not see her mother again for days and became sick with worry. Rosja had told her that if she did not reveal the code, he would kill her mother. But she knew she would never, *never* reveal the code. With the code they could trap the other paratroopers and deceive the Resistance fighters and Allied pilots. Each day, before being tortured, Hannah asked God to help Mama somehow find a way to escape from Hungary. But on June 23 that hope was dashed when Hannah learned from a guard that Mama had been in the same prison for weeks!

The very afternoon that Rosja had told her to go home, Mama had been arrested by the Arrow Cross waiting at her house. They had slapped Mama and then had roughly brought her back to the prison.

Hannah ached to see her mother again. She had to think of a way of communicating with her. But how? Hannah was in solitary confinement, and her window was nothing more than a tiny, horizontal hole near the ceiling. Lying on her back in her cell, she stared for a long time up at the miserable window. It was impossible for her to look out . . . or was it?

The next morning Hannah got an idea. A sympathetic guard, Hulda, who was really a prisoner assigned to do prison chores, lent Hannah a chair each morning to use as a washstand for her bowl of water. The chair had to be returned in fifteen minutes. Hannah acted quickly. She lifted the rickety table and placed it on her bed, then balanced the chair on top of that. Carefully she climbed on the bed, the table, and finally the chair, holding onto the inside ledge of the high window for support. It worked! She could see directly into the cell across from her own. She could see her mother among the other prisoners!

Hannah slipped a note to Hulda to give to Mama. "Look out your window tomorrow morning."

The next morning Hannah climbed up to the chair on the table on the bed and peered out. Across the prison yard she saw Mama smiling and waving.

Hannah waved back and laughed. She blew kisses, and then very slowly outlined letters in the air with her finger.

"Are you well, Mama?" she asked.

Her mother answered, "Yes."

Hannah replied she, too, was fine. They had not tortured her the last few days.

Noticing the felt Star of David sewn to the other prisoners' shabby dresses, Hannah asked Mama, "Why do you and the other women have to wear the yellow star on your clothes?"

Tracing letters in the air, Hannah's mother explained, "The law now says that all Jews must wear the yellow Star of David to identify them as Jews. Why don't you have to wear one?"

Hannah answered, "I am no longer considered a Hungarian citizen, so I'm not bound by such laws."

Hannah's mother's cellmates watched this correspondence with interest. One of the women wrote in the air to Hannah, "You are lucky not to be branded."

As an answer, Hannah drew an enormous Star of David with her finger in the dust of the window.

Hannah's star remained on her cell window for many weeks. It became the symbol of Jewish pride and inspiration to the prisoners. Until the warden ordered the window washed, the star remained. In the day the summer sun shone on the star, and at night the dull light from Hannah's cell illuminated the star for all to see as a beacon in the darkness.

thirteen-

Hungary 1944

Each morning Hannah was taken by prison van to the Gestapo prison on Schwab Hill to be interrogated, but she was no longer tortured. After she was brought back to the Conti Street prison, Hulda would try to arrange a brief meeting between Hannah and her mother: two minutes in the same bathroom, a minute in the prison yard, a half minute in the corridor.

Before Hannah left for Schwab Hill, she cut out letters from scraps of paper and held the letters up to the window to communicate with her mother. If she heard a guard coming, she would jump down from her homemade ladder and hide the paper letters under her mattress. Often days, even weeks, went by when she dared not display the paper messages.

On July 17, Hannah's twenty-third birthday, Hulda brought Hannah a parcel. It was from Mama! Hannah opened the crudely wrapped little bundle and stared at the unexpected luxuries before her. There was a little jar of orange marmalade, sent to Mama from a Christian friend outside prison.

And there were birthday donations from Mama's cellmates: a handkerchief, a sliver of soap, a piece of sponge.

Immediately, Hannah wrote a thank-you note to Mama and the other women. "The marmalade is especially marvelous," she wrote. "It pleases me so much because it reminds me of Eretz with its beautiful orange groves."

Hannah could not forget Palestine. In the bleak, cruel prison, where each day Jewish prisoners were pulled from their cells and deported to concentration camps, Hannah kept the dream of a Jewish homeland alive. She began her paper messages again, teaching her mother and the others Hebrew in her window-to-window classroom. Whenever she was taken out of solitary confinement, she found a way to talk of Palestine to the prisoners without the guards knowing. She told stories about the land, her own experiences. She spoke of S'dot Yam and its glittering blue sea. She taught Zionist songs, Zionist history, and made dreams for those who could no longer make their own.

Homeless children on the way to the death camps passed through the prison. Hannah hugged them, kissed them, played with them when the guards looked the other way. She told them the stories her father had once told her. Hulda brought Hannah bits of rag, paper, and crayons. Remembering the little dolls she had once made with Fini Mama, Hannah sat in her damp cell and created little rag and paper dolls in exotic colorful costumes. She made Gypsy dolls, ballerina dolls, Chinese dolls, and her favorite—kibbutznik dolls shouldering hoes and shovels. She gave them freely to the children, realizing that these dolls would be their last toys.

One morning, while she was making dolls and paper flowers and her cell was bathed in a cool and quiet shade, Hannah saw a strange bright light flashing on the ceiling. She sat on her cot and stared at the light for some time before she realized its meaning. Someone was flashing a message to her!

Hannah translated the short and long flashes into Morse

code. Yoel Palgi! He and Peretz Goldstein were in the same prison three floors below her cell. Hannah understood his signals.

"I waited for you at the Great Synagogue and later at the cathedral. I went every day and waited for you, hoping you'd come. I, too, have been tortured here, but still I am not giving up hope."

Hannah knew what Yoel meant. It was almost September, and the Nazis were doing badly. The Russian Red Army had already taken Yugoslavia and southern Hungary. It would be only a matter of days until they reached Budapest. Every day Budapest was being bombed. Best of all, Horthy had appointed a new prime minister, General Géza Lakatos. Horthy, fed up with the German Nazis controlling Hungary, hoped that this moderate general would turn Hungary to the winning Allied side and so end the war in Hungary.

That afternoon, when the sun lay on Hannah's side of the prison, she used her mirror to flash a message back. She told him she was encouraged by the political moves in Hungary. "I will never give up hope," she said. "One day we will return to Palestine."

Hannah's spirits remained high. Her window continued to be the prison information and education center. She relayed news of the war, meanings of Hebrew words, and messages of hope. To those who awaited sentencing, she flashed her motto, "Never give up the struggle!"

As the Red Army got closer and closer to Budapest, the prison rules slackened. Many of the soldiers ran away or, fearing prisoner vengeance after the war, began to treat the prisoners more humanely. Hannah found it easier to snatch a few moments with Mama in the prison yard, and her trips to Schwab Hill for interrogation became less frequent. An attempt had been made on Hitler's life, and when Hannah heard the news from a guard, she flashed it to the others. "The war will soon be over," everyone whispered. "The end is near!"

On September 12, Hannah's mother and other prisoners were taken in a huge van to the Kistarcsa internment camp. Here they were allowed more freedom. They could write as many letters as they wanted, walk around inside the fences, and even receive visitors. Then on Yom Kippur, everyone in Kistarcsa was released.

Hannah's mother went to see her sister, who was living in a Yellow Star House. After a day, she went back to the prison to see Hannah and was allowed a ten-minute visit.

Mama pulled out the little gifts she had brought with her, donated by friends and relatives. Hannah was delighted with the rare treats: a lump of cheese, fruit, a sweater, underwear, paper, and pencils. Then Mama gave her the most precious gift of all—Hannah's own little sewing kit that Mama and Papa had given her as a child. Looking at the little kit, still complete with colored threads and assorted needles, Hannah cried. She remembered the sweet hours with Fini Mama making clothes, handkerchiefs, and bookmarks.

"Was there ever such a time," Hannah asked in wonderment, "of childhood and carefree happiness?"

Mama and Hannah hugged each other. Then they realized they had better talk quickly since they had only five minutes left to visit.

"What else would you like, Aniko?" Mama asked.

"Bring me books. We're allowed to read now, and what I would especially like is a Hebrew Bible."

"Is that all you want?" asked Mama.

"No, Mama, I need warmer clothes. It's so cold in my cell."

The five minutes were almost up. Hurriedly Hannah told Mama, "I'm going to be tried soon. I need a lawyer to defend me. Find me a lawyer soon—as soon as possible."

Mama promised she would, and then it was time to leave. But before she left she showed Hannah a mysterious note that had arrived at the house of her Christian friend. The note was addressed to Hannah and contained a large amount of money to buy "Hannah whatever she needed." Hannah read the note and at once her eyes sparkled. "It's from Reuven!" He had gone back and retrieved her poem and now had found the way to send her money. She was filled with happiness and gratitude that he was free and trying to help her! One day she would tell Mama all about him and Yoel and her life in Yugoslavia. But now Mama had to leave.

Hannah's mother spent the next weeks feverishly trying to get help for Hannah. Jews were allowed on the streets for only two hours a day, so she had to work fast. Every day she went to the Zionist Organization to seek advice and help. But they were slow and misguided. They said they could do nothing for Hannah. In the first week of October, Hannah's mother hired a young lawyer, Dr. Szélecsenyi, to defend her daughter.

Dr. Szélecsenyi visited Hannah on October 13. Afterward, he told her mother what to expect.

"She is very brave," he said. "Not one man in a thousand would have attempted what she did. I have great admiration for her. But if she goes to trial, she will definitely be convicted." Mama's frightened face made him say quickly, "I have no idea what the sentence will be—maybe five years, maybe two, maybe seven. But this is not important because the war is almost over. Then the political prisoners will be released."

"Will I be able to see my daughter?" Catherine Szenes asked.

"Not until after the trial on October twenty-eighth," Dr. Szélecsenyi said. "That is the rule of the judge advocate, Captain Simon."

Hannah's mother waited.

On October 15, the Lakatos government fell to the Arrow Cross leader Ferenc Szálasi. With Szálasi as prime minister, the remaining Jews in Hungary were doomed. Cooperating with Germany's top Nazi in Budapest, Adolf Eichmann, Szálasi unleashed all the brutal sadism of the Arrow Crossers onto the Jews. At once, hordes of Arrow Crossers burst into Yellow Star Homes, Jewish hospitals, and orphanages and began massacring everyone in sight. They rounded up men and women and marched them to Margaret Bridge, where they were shot and thrown into the cold Danube. In the chilling beginnings of the Budapest winter lay 20,000 Jewish bodies to be cleared away. The damp air stank with death.

Eichmann planned the total destruction of all Jews in Hungary. Every day thousands of families were packed into freight trains going to the German death camps. When the trains proved inadequate even for this task, Eichmann and Szálasi announced that 27,000 Jewish men and women would be forced to walk the hundred miles to Germany to work as slaves. Without food, warm clothes, or shelter, most of them died on the way or were left to starve in ditches. The roads were lined with corpses.

In this hellish and hateful time, Hannah's mother made her way to Miklós Horthy prison on October 28. Covering her yellow-star patch on her black coat with her handbag, she entered the little antechamber of the courtroom. Underneath the sign that read HANNAH SZENES AND ACCOMPLICES, she sat on the bench and waited, hoping to catch a glimpse of her daughter after the trial. While crowds of Arrow Crossers with submachine guns milled about the prison and Russian bombs boomed at the outskirts of the city, Hannah, the stubborn Jewish prisoner accused of high treason, was led into the courtroom.

fourteen-

Hungary 1944

The president of the tribunal asked, "Hannah Szenes, are you guilty or not guilty?"

"I am *not* guilty, your honor," Hannah replied. "May I have the right to speak?"

"Permission to speak granted," the president said.

Hannah stood up and looked squarely at the judge (Count Gero Ladislas) and the judge advocate, Captain Simon. Now she would speak the truth—make them know the truth. She must not fail. "I do not admit treason to my native land, Hungary. My father was a Hungarian author who left an inheritance to me and to others—he taught us to have faith in the good. But when I grew up, the streets of the city taught me that as a Jew I had no place in this country. One by one the politicians voted for race discrimination, deprivation of human rights, the cruelty of the Middle Ages."

Hannah felt herself trembling at the force of her own words. A hush had fallen over the courtroom—they were listening. With growing courage, Hannah went on. "I understood then that I have no homeland. You canceled my citizenship with your hate. I went away to build a homeland, a Jewish home-land, a true homeland. And this regime, which had deluded the people for an entire generation, brought upon them the worst catastrophe: it dragged Hungary into the war, and on the wrong side—the side of evil."

"Don't let the traitor speak!" someone shouted, and Hannah heard others shouting in agreement.

"She is speaking lies!" someone else said.

Hannah looked around at the Hungarian Nazis, the Arrow Crossers, who crowded the courtroom. She could not stop now. She *must not* stop. No matter how unpopular and sui-cidal her talk, she would go on. She admitted her crime of spying and that she had come to save Jews, but she did not admit she was wrong. "It is not I who am the traitor! They are the traitors who brought this calamity upon our people and upon themselves! I implore you, don't add to your crimes. Save my people."

The judges were shocked by the young Jew's passionate words. Never had they seen such a brave and eloquent woman. They were confused and upset. They postponed their deci-sion. Hannah's sentence, they said, would not be passed for another eight days—on November 4.

Still excited from her speech, Hannah was led out of the courtroom and into the antechamber. There, she saw her mother's aged, worried face.

"Don't worry, Mama," Hannah said, hugging her closely. "The judges were impressed by my speech." Then Hannah assured Mama that Dr. Szélecsenyi, her lawyer, had also spo-ken very well.

But no words could console Mama. "I don't like this delay. I don't like it, Aniko."

"Mama, the delay means *nothing*! Anyway, while the war continues, I won't be released. Then afterward, we'll all be freed! Besides, Mama, *you* are now in more danger than I am. Look at you, covering your yellow star and going out into the streets. Why don't your friends help you? Why don't you go into hiding? Please, Mama, try to escape!"

"I can't escape—not yet," Mama answered. "Not until your case is settled."

"I'll muddle through somehow," Hannah said, trying to sound very brave. "But you *must* disappear—go into hiding. I won't have any peace if you're this careless!"

The guard signaled that it was time for Mrs. Szenes to leave. He told her she could obtain a visitor's pass to see her daughter again on October 30. Then he led Hannah away, back to her prison cell. Mama watched Hannah, flanked by two guards, walk across the wide prison yard until she disappeared from view.

The days that followed were filled with bombs exploding and artillery fire. Houses were blown up, buildings crumbled, trees fell everywhere, blocking roads and streets. And in the prison, Hannah's small window rattled loudly with each explosion. The Russians were on the edges of the city. Everyone knew it would be only a matter of days until Budapest fell to the Allies. The prisoners were hopeful. Already the prison officials were burning court records, letting many prisoners leave, and fleeing themselves.

By the end of October, the judges who had tried Hannah had fled the country. Confusion reigned. Hannah's conviction date was postponed as a new judge had to be appointed.

Death and destruction were everywhere. Nearly 6 million Jews in Europe had already been killed. Only in Hungary were a sizeable number of Jews still alive, all in Budapest. But while Hannah languished in prison, Eichmann sent a letter to Heinrich Himmler, head of the Nazi secret police:

> The complete liquidation of Hungary's Jews is an accomplished fact. Technical details will only take a few more days in Budapest.

The ghetto of Yellow Star Houses was circled by guards with machine guns and, beyond them, high walls of barbed wire. Typhus raged throughout the ghetto, in the deportation camps, and on the freight trains heading to the concentration camps. Those who were sick were clubbed or shot to death.

Suicide was commonplace. As the brakemen waved lanterns for the trains to roll, people threw themselves on the tracks to escape the suffering ahead. The frosty air of early November was filled with the sickening stench of disease and death.

Alone in her cell, Hannah shivered from the bitter cold. On the small table lay scraps of paper with unfinished poems. On one scrap was scribbled only "I loved the warm sunlight." Hannah had grown ghostly thin from the cruel food ration, and she now had a bad cough. The hope she had tried to give her mother was leaving her. She had not heard from her mother or anybody else in days. Yoel was somewhere in the same prison, but it had been weeks since she last communicated with him and she had no idea whether he was still alive.

As the ear-shattering booms of the Russian bombs echoed through the dank prison, Hannah thought of those she loved. Only George among them was safe, having escaped from France to Palestine. Evi and her family had already died in Auschwitz. Other relatives were trapped in Yellow Star Houses to meet the same fate. And Mama, brave Mama, walked the streets freely, endangering her own life to save Hannah's.

Hannah paced back and forth in her cell. At last she sat down. She looked at the scraps of paper and read the last poem she had written—more than six months ago.

> One—two—three . . .
>   eight feet long,
> Two strides across, the rest is dark . . .
> Life hangs over me like a question mark.
>
> One—two—three . . .
>   maybe another week,
> Or next month may still find me here,
> But death, I feel, is very near.
>
> I could have been
>   twenty-three next July;
> I gambled on what mattered most,
> The dice were cast. I lost.

A few days later, on a cold, dark morning when leaden clouds hung over Budapest like a shroud, Hannah's mother waited in Judge Advocate Captain Simon's office to receive the visitor's pass to see her daughter. At the same time, Captain Simon suddenly entered Hannah's cell.

"Hannah Szenes, you have been sentenced to death. Do you wish to ask for clemency?"

"Sentenced to death? No, I wish to appeal. Bring me my lawyer."

"You cannot appeal. You may ask for clemency."

Hannah's mind raced. "I was tried before a lower tribunal. I know I have the right to appeal."

"There are no appeals. I repeat, do you or do you not wish to ask for clemency?"

"Clemency—from you? Do you think I'm going to plead with hangmen and murderers? I shall *never* ask you for mercy."

"In that case, prepare to die!" Captain Simon said. "You may write farewell letters. But hurry. We shall carry out the sentence one hour from now."

Hannah sat down on her cot, and for several moments she could not move. She stared at the brick wall in front of her. The deep gray light of the sky outside entered her cell. She had faced another death under a sky like this many years ago.

Fini Mama had said, "Now is the time for you to be strong. Remember, you are great children."

I have failed in my mission, Hannah thought, but my life has been good.

"Papa, I've learned I can write."

"On the whole, Miss Szenes, I find you talented. Yes, I think you will become a writer..."

"Grow up little chick, grow up and be strong."

Hannah Szenes- 101

Hannah roused herself from her memories. She asked the guard for paper and a pen and feverishly began to write. First, she wrote to Yoel and Peretz.

> Continue on the way; don't be deterred. Continue the struggle till the end, until the day of liberty comes, the day of victory for our people.

Then Hannah wrote to S'dot Yam, to George, and, on the little scrap of paper she had left, she wrote to Mama.

There were so many things she wanted to say. If only Mama were here she could hug her, kiss her, and tell her how sorry she was for causing her this sadness. But Mama was not here and time was running out, so she wrote:

> Dearest Mother:
>
> I don't know what to say—only this: a million thanks, and forgive me, if you can. You know so well why words aren't necessary. With love forever.
>
> Your Daughter

An hour passed, and no one came to get her. Finally, at 10:00 A.M. Captain Simon returned. He ordered the soldiers to take her down to the prison yard. He was both nervous and exultant. He had lied to her. No sentence had been passed. Now he was putting her to death by his own wish. He would rid himself of this proud, insolent girl who had branded the Arrow Crossers as evil. He would do away with her for good.

As Captain Simon left to tell Mrs. Szenes why no visitor's pass would be granted to her, two soldiers hammered a wooden post into the sandbox. Next, they tied Hannah's hands behind her back and strapped her to the post. From a small nearby table with its crucifix, one of the soldiers brought her a blindfold. Hannah looked into his eyes and shook her head. She would not wear it.

As the firing squad raised their rifles and took aim, she stared at them and beyond them—to the dim sunlight of that morning's sky.

Three months after Hannah's execution, the Russian army liberated Budapest. By that time, the once beautiful city lay in ruins from the bombings. Death and destruction were everywhere. On nearly every street corner lay piles of human corpses, the bitter February wind carrying the odor of decay. Bits of cannon and artillery were scattered amid the rubble of ruined houses and burnt-out cars.

Catherine Szenes, who had sought refuge in a convent, made her way to her home in Rose Hill. To get to her house, she had to crawl across craters in the street, climb over broken doors, and step carefully around blown-out windows. At last, she found her way to Bimbo Street.

The house was still there but heavily damaged. Parts of the roof were missing, and the iron gate was gone. She opened the front door and walked inside.

All the cupboards and closets were wide open—dirty and empty. The furniture had been stolen, and the curtains lay on the floor, trampled in the dirt.

In the parlor the glass bookcases had been broken and emptied. Torn books swam in puddles of rainwater. Béla's plays and poetry lay in a white mess of plaster that had fallen from the ceiling. Among the mess, Catherine found a photograph.

With a grieving heart, Catherine stared at the picture of Hannah taken in Palestine—the smiling face of a young woman in a summer dress, picking flowers in a faraway homeland. Beside the muddied photograph lay Hannah's letters from Palestine, her stories, and her poems. They were torn, smeared with mud, and buried in plaster—buried as if forever.

epilogue-

Although Hannah's life was cruelly ended in the grim yard of a military prison, the spirit of her life—its courage and hope—remained to light the way for those still alive. Among the last pockets of Jewish Resistance fighters, in the rotting prison cells and in the bombed, death-ridden ghettos, the story of the woman who left the safety of Palestine to save Jews in Europe was told from survivor to survivor.

By the time the war ended in Hungary in February 1945, over 450,000 Jews—70 percent of the Jewish population of Greater Hungary—had been annihilated.

At the time when great nations hesitated to interfere, when churches remained silent, and when many Jews themselves were paralyzed by fear, Hannah's actions loomed extraordinary. She was young, inexperienced, and often foolhardy, but she tried. "I'm conscious-stricken that I have it so good and easy here while others are suffering," Hannah wrote in her diary. In the end, her responsibility to the oppressed made her a martyr. But, more important, in a time of pervasive inhumanity, it marked her as human.

Hannah did not live to see the land she loved become a nation, but that nation has shown its love for her. Today in Israel, nearly every schoolchild can recite "Blessed Is the Match." Numerous plays and books have been written about Hannah. Thirty-two streets are named "Hannah Szenes," as well as a forest, two farming settlements, and a refugee ship.

Overlooking Jerusalem, in the highest of the Judean hills, Hannah is buried. There, in the National Military Cemetery, a circle is etched into the earth. Within the circle, in the shape of a "V," lie the graves of the seven parachutists who did not return. On each headstone is carved a parachute.

Throughout the year, visitors place flowers at Hannah's grave. And when the visitors leave, winding their way down the hill, the memory of Hannah does not end. Her words are read and re-read in countries around the world, inspiring ever-new generations with their gentle wisdom and hope— Hannah's song of light.

> *There are stars whose radiance is visible on earth though they have long been extinct. There are people whose brilliance continues to light the world though they are no longer among the living. These lights are particularly bright when the night is dark. They light the way for Mankind.*
>
> *—Hannah Szenes*